STECK-VAUGHN
Level B

 W9-AZO-574

LANGUAGE EXERCISES

FOR ADULTS

Betty Jones
Saranna Moeller
Cynthia T. Strauch

Consultants

John Ritter
Master Teacher
Oregon Women's Correctional Center
Salem, Oregon

Dannette S. Queen
Adult Education
New York City Board of Education
Bronx, New York

STECK-VAUGHN
COMPANY
ELEMENTARY · SECONDARY · ADULT · LIBRARY

Acknowledgments

Executive Editor: Diane Sharpe
Supervising Editor: Stephanie Muller
Project Editor: Patricia Claney
Design Manager: Richard Balsam

Illustrations: Rosemarie Fox Hicks and Michael Krone
Photography: Cooke Photographic, Bob Daemmrich, Phyllis Liedeker, James Minor, David Omer, Park Street, Rick Williams
Stock Photography: p.25 a © Frank Cezus/FPG; b Courtesy Lick Observatory; p.26 a Circus World Museum, Baraboo, WI; p.29 b © Oxford Scientific Films/Animals Animals; c © Rick Smolan/Stock Boston; f © Elizabeth Hamlin/Stock Boston; p.53 n Courtesy Texas Highways; p.58 © Jose Carrillo/PhotoEdit; p.66 a © Michael Newman/PhotoEdit; p.88 © Jean-Claude Lejeune/Stock Boston; p.90 a © John Maher/Stock Boston; p.91 a © David Young Wolfe/PhotoEdit; p.103 c © D R Specker/Animals Animals; d © Stephen Dalton/Animals Animals; e © John Lei/Stock Boston.

LANGUAGE EXERCISES Series:		
Level A	Level D	Level G
Level B	Level E	Level H
Level C	Level F	Review

ISBN 0-8114-7876-9

Copyright © 1995 Steck-Vaughn Company.
All rights reserved. No part of the material protected by this copyright may be reproduced or utilized in any form or by any means, electronic or mechanical, including photocopying, recording, or by any information storage and retrieval system, without permission in writing from the copyright owner. Requests for permission to make copies of any part of the work should be mailed to: Copyright Permissions, Steck-Vaughn Company, P.O. Box 26015, Austin, TX 78755. Printed in the United States of America.

2 3 4 5 6 7 8 9 DBH 00 99 98 97 96 95

Table of Contents

Unit 1   Study Skills

Unit 2   Vocabulary

Unit 3   Sentences

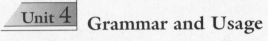
Unit 4   Grammar and Usage

Unit 5   Capitalization and Punctuation

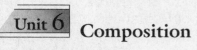

A. **Look at the photo. Follow the directions.**

1. Put an X on the apple.

2. Put an X to the right of the apple.

3. Put an X above the apple.

4. Draw a circle around the apple.

B. **Look at the map, and read the directions to Jesse's house. Then answer the questions.**

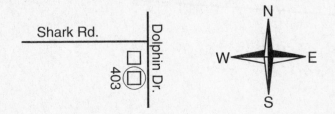

1) Go east on Shark Road.
2) Turn south on Dolphin Drive.
3) Walk down two houses to 403 Dolphin Drive.

1. What direction should you go first? _____

2. What street should you walk on first? _____

3. Which direction should you turn? _____

4. What street should you turn on? _____

5. How many houses down Dolphin Drive is Jesse's house? _____

C. Cross out the word that does not belong.

1. cup   plate   fork   pen

2. boat   car   name   train

3. tree   door   flower   bush

D. Write the words in alphabetical order.

1. Zena_____   2. door _____

   Carol_____   window _____

   Thomas_____   carpet _____

E. Underline the words that would be on the same page as the guide words.

　　　　　　day / fish

1. dear   laugh   pig   knob

2. red   sell   egg   dark

3. bait   dust   gold   map

F. Use the dictionary words to answer the questions.

bill 1. a bird's beak 　　　 2. a paper that shows 　　　　　how much you owe	**boil** to heat a liquid until 　　　 bubbles form **box** a container used for 　　　 storing things

1. What word has two meanings? _____

2. What word means "a container used for storing things"? _____

3. What does <u>boil</u> mean? _____

G. Read the words in the box. Then follow the directions.

| narrow | pan | angry | short | knew | big |

1. Write the words from the box that rhyme.

   due _____   man _____

2. Write the words from the box that mean almost the same.

   mad _____   large _____

3. Write the words from the box that mean the opposite.

   tall _____   wide _____

H. Circle the correct word to complete each sentence.

1. I went (to, too, two) the bank.

2. I am going to (hear, here) the symphony today.

3. I will meet my friends (there, their).

I. Write T before the telling sentence. Write A before the asking sentence. Write X before the group of words that is not a sentence. Circle the naming parts. Underline the action parts.

_____ 1. Am I sick?

_____ 2. To get better.

_____ 3. I bought some medicine.

J. Circle the special naming words. Underline the action words.

1. Mr. Donaldson grows his own vegetables.

2. He plants some of the vegetables in April.

K. Circle the word that best completes each sentence.

1. Rajib and I (was, were) out of town last week.

2. (We, They) went to Vancouver.

3. Rajib took (a, an) camera.

4. Rajib and I (is, are) going to show you our pictures.

L. Circle each letter that should be a capital letter. Write the correct punctuation marks for each sentence.

1. mr t r wiggins and i went to daytona beach last saturday sunday and monday

2. rhonda went to the beach last august

3. didnt she take her cat named whiskers

M. Read the paragraph. Circle the main idea, and underline the supporting details.

Julia wanted to bake her friend a cake for his birthday.

First, Julia read the recipe. Then she baked the cake.

After the cake cooled, she put frosting on it.

Below is a list of the sections on *Check What You Know* and the pages on which the skills in each section are taught. If you missed any questions, turn to the pages listed and practice the skills. Then correct the problems you missed on *Check What You Know*.

Section	Practice Page		Section	Practice Page		Section	Practice Page
Unit 1			Unit 2			Unit 5	
A	5–8		G	23–25		L	68–73, 77–79, 82
B	9		H	26–28		Unit 6	
C	11		Unit 3			M	88–90
D	13		I	34, 36–42			
E	14		Unit 4				
F	15–17		J	47–48, 50–51			
			K	53–54, 60, 62			

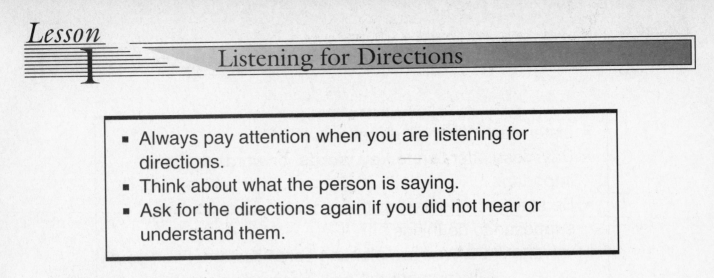

- Always pay attention when you are listening for directions.
- Think about what the person is saying.
- Ask for the directions again if you did not hear or understand them.

■ Choose a partner for this lesson. Look at the photo as your partner reads the directions to you. Then follow the directions.

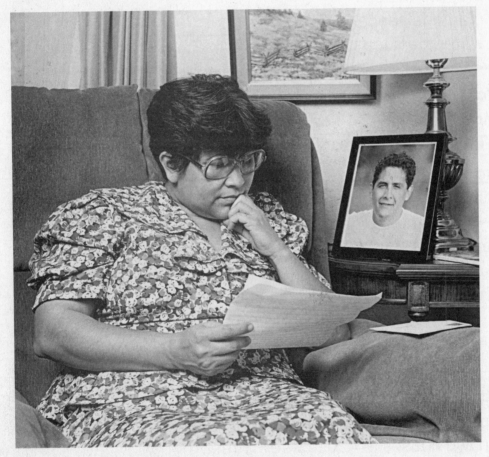

1. Put an H to the left of the woman's head.
2. Put an A above the woman's head.
3. Draw a circle around the letter.
4. Draw a circle around the photo on the table.
5. Put an X on the envelope.

Lesson 2

More Listening for Directions

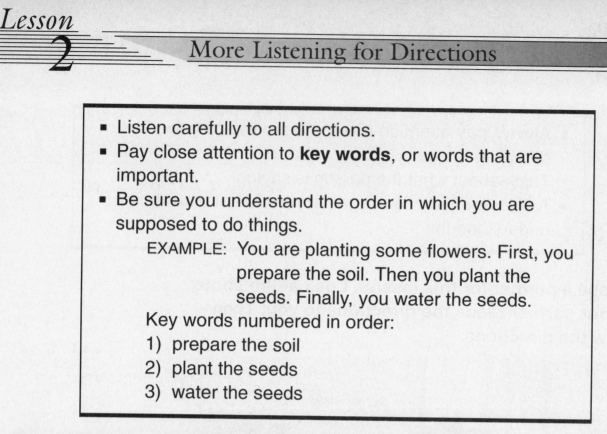

- Listen carefully to all directions.
- Pay close attention to **key words**, or words that are important.
- Be sure you understand the order in which you are supposed to do things.

    EXAMPLE: You are planting some flowers. First, you prepare the soil. Then you plant the seeds. Finally, you water the seeds.

    Key words numbered in order:
    1) prepare the soil
    2) plant the seeds
    3) water the seeds

- **Choose a partner for this lesson. Listen to the directions as your partner reads them to you. Then write the key words in the order in which they should be done.**

1. Your roommate wants you to do a few things when you get home from work. These are her directions: First, pick up the dry cleaning. Then vacuum the living room. Finally, feed the cat.

    1) _____

    2) _____

    3) _____

2. Your friend invites you to his house. Here are his directions: Go south on Red Road. Turn west on Green Street. Walk down two houses to 4202 Green Street.

    1) _____

    2) _____

    3) _____

■ **Read and follow the directions. Write the words that are in the dark boxes.**

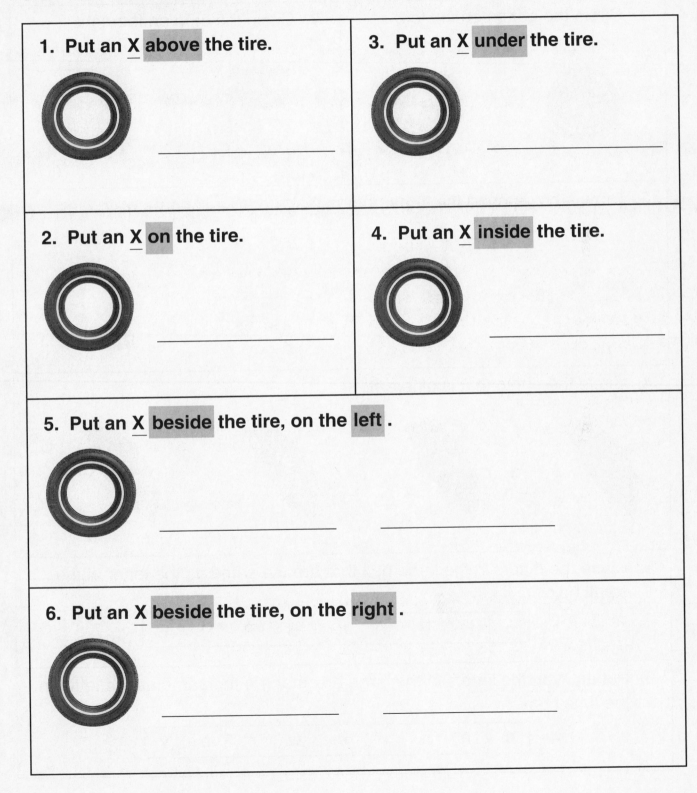

1. Put an X above the tire.

3. Put an X under the tire.

2. Put an X on the tire.

4. Put an X inside the tire.

5. Put an X beside the tire, on the left .

6. Put an X beside the tire, on the right .

- **Read the sentences. Follow the directions.**

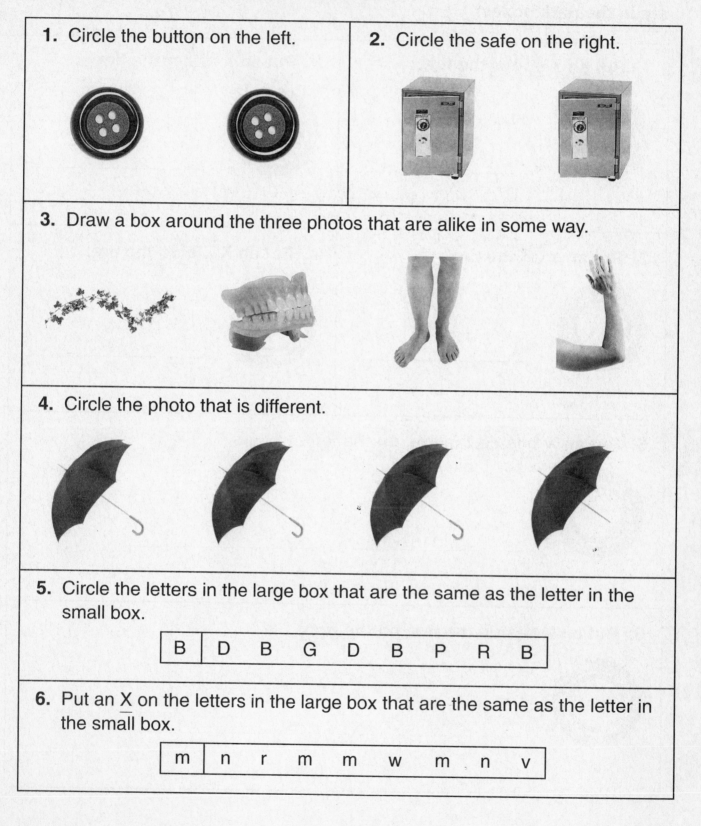

1. Circle the button on the left.

2. Circle the safe on the right.

3. Draw a box around the three photos that are alike in some way.

4. Circle the photo that is different.

5. Circle the letters in the large box that are the same as the letter in the small box.

   | B | D B G D B P R B |

6. Put an X on the letters in the large box that are the same as the letter in the small box.

   | m | n r m m w m n v |

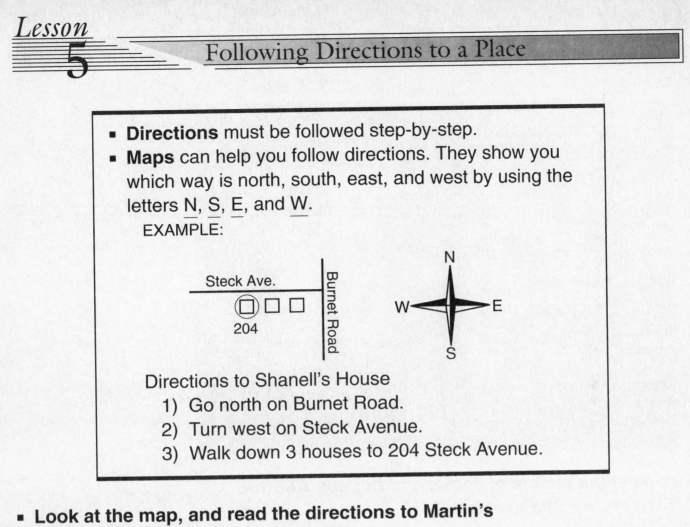

- **Directions** must be followed step-by-step.
- **Maps** can help you follow directions. They show you which way is north, south, east, and west by using the letters N, S, E, and W.

EXAMPLE:

Directions to Shanell's House

1) Go north on Burnet Road.
2) Turn west on Steck Avenue.
3) Walk down 3 houses to 204 Steck Avenue.

- **Look at the map, and read the directions to Martin's house. Then answer the questions.**

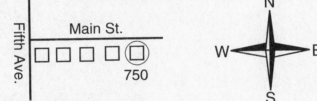

1) Go south on Fifth Avenue.
2) Turn east on Main Street.
3) Walk down 5 houses to 750 Main Street.

1. What direction should you go first? _____

2. What street should you walk on first? _____

3. What direction should you go next? _____

4. What street should you be on? _____

5. How many houses down Main Street is Martin's house? _____

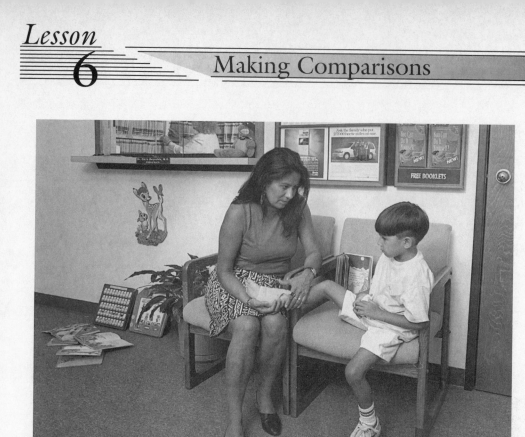

■ **Look at the picture of Jackie and her son Andrew.
Then answer the questions.**

1. Who is older? _____

2. Who is younger? _____

3. Who is shorter? _____

4. Who is taller? _____

5. Who has shorter hair? _____

6. Who has longer hair? _____

7. Who is wearing the shirt with longer sleeves? _____

8. Who is wearing the shirt with the shorter sleeves? _____

9. Who is closer to the door? _____

10. Who is farther from the door? _____

■ **Cross out the word that does not belong.**

1. red   blue   white   ~~turtle~~
2. walk   drive   dog   run
3. computer   Kim   Terry   Susan
4. book   sink   pencil   paper
5. cat   fish   raccoon   woman
6. happy   popcorn   sad   angry
7. breakfast   lunch   candle   supper
8. milk   water   juice   mud
9. sock   chair   table   bed
10. above   under   blue   beside

■ **Read the words in the box. Write each word in the correct group.**

apple	Jenny	bread	rice	potato	cheese
Andy	type	Vince	sing	Dennis	dance
eat	write	Lupe	talk	Rudy	grapes

Foods	**Names**	**Actions**
apple	Andy	eat

- **Write the missing letters.**

A   B   C   D

- **Write the letter that comes next.**

1. S   T   U

2. H   I   ____

3. B   C   ____

4. P   Q   ____

5. M   N   ____

6. K   L   ____

7. V   W   ____

8. E   F   ____

9. X   Y   ____

10. O   P   ____

11. D   E   ____

12. J   K   ____

- **Write the letter that comes in the middle.**

1. J   K   L

2. E   ____   G

3. Q   ____   S

4. F   ____   H

5. W   ____   Y

6. C   ____   E

7. T   ____   V

8. M   ____   O

9. S   ____   U

10. A   ____   C

11. L   ____   N

12. D   ____   F

- **Write the letter that comes before.**

1. A   B   C

2. ____   T   U

3. ____   N   O

4. ____   X   Y

5. ____   J   K

6. ____   F   G

7. ____   L   M

8. ____   H   I

9. ____   Q   R

10. ____   S   T

11. ____   V   W

12. ____   K   L

- **Number the words in alphabetical order. Then write the words in the right order.**

1.

_2_ bag   1. _air_

_1_ air   2. _bag_

_3_ car   3. _car_

6.

____ neck   1. ____

____ owl   2. ____

____ mail   3. ____

2.

____ tool   1. ____

____ sea   2. ____

____ rock   3. ____

7.

____ well   1. ____

____ us   2. ____

____ very   3. ____

3.

____ egg   1. ____

____ fish   2. ____

____ dog   3. ____

8.

____ yes   1. ____

____ zoo   2. ____

____ x-ray   3. ____

4.

____ hat   1. ____

____ ice   2. ____

____ gate   3. ____

9.

____ pan   1. ____

____ oak   2. ____

____ nail   3. ____

5.

____ joke   1. ____

____ lake   2. ____

____ king   3. ____

10.

____ quit   1. ____

____ sun   2. ____

____ rug   3. ____

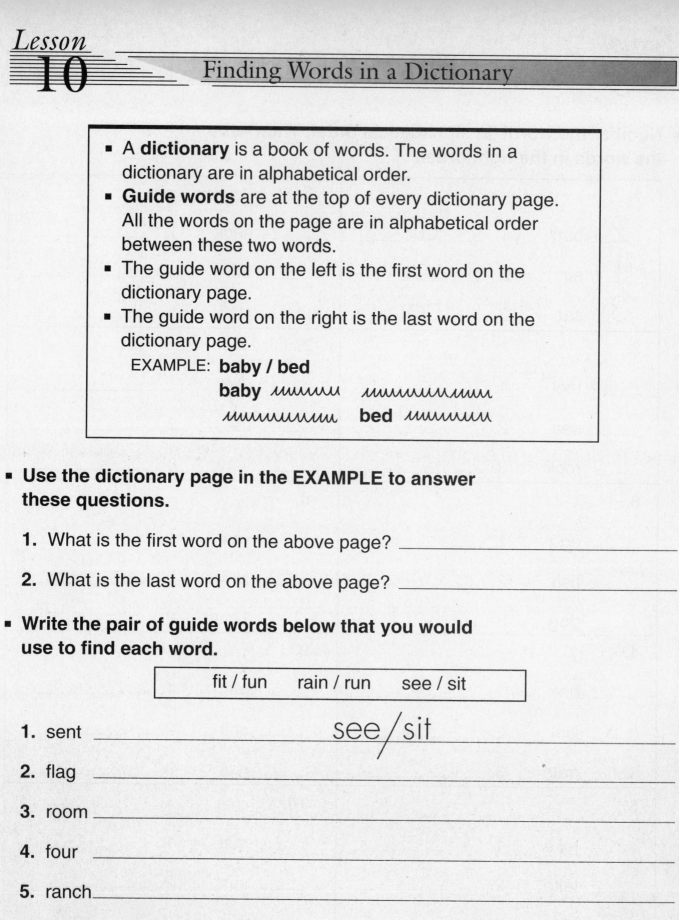

- A **dictionary** is a book of words. The words in a dictionary are in alphabetical order.
- **Guide words** are at the top of every dictionary page. All the words on the page are in alphabetical order between these two words.
- The guide word on the left is the first word on the dictionary page.
- The guide word on the right is the last word on the dictionary page.

    EXAMPLE: **baby / bed**

    baby ～～～ ～～～～～～
    ～～～～～～ **bed** ～～～～

- **Use the dictionary page in the EXAMPLE to answer these questions.**

    1. What is the first word on the above page? _____

    2. What is the last word on the above page? _____

- **Write the pair of guide words below that you would use to find each word.**

    | fit / fun   rain / run   see / sit |

    1. sent _____ *see/sit* _____

    2. flag _____

    3. room _____

    4. four _____

    5. ranch _____

    6. sheep _____

- A dictionary shows how to spell words.
- A dictionary tells what words mean.

many   a large number

middle   in between

neighbor   someone who lives in the next house

new   never used before

noise   a sound that is loud

open   not shut

paw   the foot of an animal

return   to go back

- **Use the dictionary words to answer the questions.**

1. What word means "in between"? _____

2. What word means "the foot of an animal"? _____

3. What word means "not shut"? _____

4. What word means "a sound that is loud"? _____

5. What word means "a large number"? _____

6. What word means "someone who lives in the next house"?

_____

7. What does <u>return</u> mean? _____

8. What does <u>new</u> mean?

_____

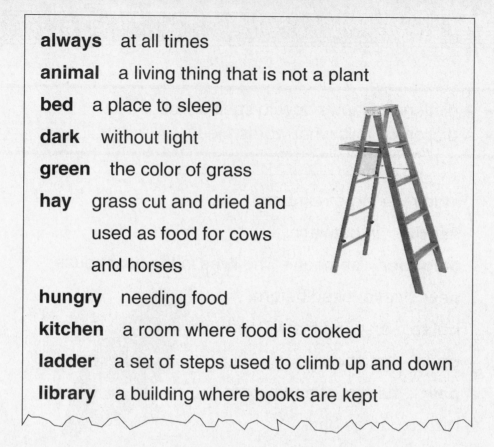

always at all times

animal a living thing that is not a plant

bed a place to sleep

dark without light

green the color of grass

hay grass cut and dried and
used as food for cows
and horses

hungry needing food

kitchen a room where food is cooked

ladder a set of steps used to climb up and down

library a building where books are kept

- **Use the dictionary words to answer the questions.
  Write <u>yes</u> or <u>no</u> on the lines.**

1. Is <u>hay</u> something that alligators eat? _____

2. Is the sunrise <u>always</u> in the morning? _____

3. Is a <u>bed</u> a place for swimming? _____

4. Is grass <u>green</u>? _____

5. Is a flower an <u>animal</u>? _____

6. Can you use a <u>ladder</u> to climb to the roof? _____

7. Is it <u>dark</u> outside at night? _____

8. Is a <u>library</u> a place for food? _____

9. Are you <u>hungry</u> after having lunch? _____

10. Is the room you sleep in called a <u>kitchen</u>? _____

> - Some words have more than one meaning.
>   EXAMPLE: **pet** 1. animal kept as a friend
>   2. to stroke
>   Ms. Watkins has a new **pet**. (meaning 1)
>   Mr. Jenkins loves to **pet** his dog. (meaning 2)

- **Read the meanings. Circle the first meaning. Draw a line under the second meaning.**

cold 1. not warm 2. a sickness of

the nose and throat

tie 1. to fasten together with string

2. a cloth worn around the neck

wave 1. moving water 2. to move the

hands back and forth as a greeting

- **Choose the correct word from above to complete each sentence. Write the number of the dictionary meaning that goes with each sentence.**

1. You need to _____ tie _____ your shoelaces.   1

2. Angela gave Dan a new _____ for his birthday.   _____

3. A huge _____ rolled toward the sandy beach.   _____

4. I always _____ to my friends at work.   _____

5. Put on a coat if you feel _____.   _____

6. Anthony had a _____ and didn't go to work.   _____

- The **table of contents** is a list at the beginning of a book. It shows the titles and page numbers of what is in the book.

Table of Contents

- **Answer these questions.**

1. What is this book about? _____

2. On what pages can you read about vegetables? _____

3. On what pages can you read about the parts of a plant? _____

4. On what pages can you read about trees? _____

5. What can you read about on page 24? _____

6. What can you read about on page 30? _____

7. On what pages can you read about poisonous plants? _____

8. On what page can you read about protecting plants? _____

9. What can you read about on page 17? _____

10. What can you read about on page 26? _____

- **Choose a partner. Look at each photo as your partner reads the directions to you. Then follow the directions.**

  1. Put an X on the saw.

     Draw a circle around the hat.

     Put an X above the hat.

     Draw a box around the saw.

- **Choose a partner. Listen to the directions as your partner reads them to you. Then write the key words in the order in which they should be done.**

  1. A news reporter says that there is a bad storm coming to your area. Here are his directions: Expect the storm in an hour. Be alert for flash floods. Stay tuned to find out which roads will be closed.

     1) _____

     2) _____

     3) _____

- **Look at the map, and read the directions to Jesse's house. Then answer the questions.**

  1) Go south on Bell Road.
  2) Turn east on April Drive.
  3) Walk down 3 houses to 104 April Drive.

  1. What direction do you go first? _____

  2. What street do you turn east on? _____

  3. How many houses down April Drive is Jesse's house? _____

- **Find the word that does not belong. Cross it out.**

  1. above   help   inside   under

  2. older   taller   longer   read

- **Number the words in alphabetical order. Then write the words in the right order.**

  1. __1__ almost   <u>almost</u>   **3.** _____ point _____

        _____ peanut _____   _____ and _____

        _____ hot _____   _____ town _____

  2. _____ zipper _____   **4.** _____ track _____

        _____ you _____   _____ wear _____

        _____ teach _____   _____ voice _____

- **Circle the word that would be on the same page as the guide words. Write the word.**

  flash / keep

  1. job   away   bark   sell   _____

  2. barn   hard   dollar   eight   _____

- **Use the dictionary words to answer the questions.**

orange	a round fruit
poor	without any money
room	part of a house

  1. What word means "without any money"? _____

  2. What word is a fruit? _____

20

- **Look at the photo. It shows Mr. and Mrs. Mendoza making dinner.**

- **Now read and follow the directions.**

   1. Write Mr. on the man.

   2. Write Mrs. on the woman.

   3. Put an X on the pot that has food cooking in it.

   4. Draw a circle around the spice rack.

   5. Put an X to the left of the basket that is hanging on the wall.

   6. Write stove on the stove.

- **Write the words on the lines under Foods or Kitchen Items.**

| carrots | knife | meat | potatoes | spoon | pot |

Foods

_____

_____

_____

Kitchen Items

_____

_____

_____

- **Read the meanings. Write the number of the meaning that goes with each underlined word.**

bark   1. the sound a dog makes

       2. hard outside covering of a tree

_____ **1.** The <u>bark</u> of the tree was smooth.

_____ **2.** We heard the dog <u>bark</u>.

- **Answer the questions. Use the table of contents.**

<table>
<tr><td colspan="2" align="center">Table of Contents</td></tr>
<tr><td>How to Become a Writer... 4</td><td>Poetry ....15</td></tr>
<tr><td>Fiction Books.................... 6</td><td>Magazine Articles ....18</td></tr>
<tr><td>Nonfiction Books.............. 8</td><td>Newspaper Articles............25</td></tr>
<tr><td>Short Stories....................13</td><td>Scripts for Plays and TV....32</td></tr>
</table>

1. What is this book about? _____

2. On what pages can you read about writing short stories? _____

3. On what page can you read about writing scripts? _____

4. What can you read about on page 6? _____

5. What can you read about on page 25? _____

- **Write each list of words in alphabetical order.**

1. bake _____

     dish _____

     face _____

     airplane _____

2. gold _____

     moon _____

     pond _____

     lake _____

> ■ Words that end with the same sound are called **rhyming words**.
>   EXAMPLES: man — fan   seat — meat   book — look

■ **Find a rhyming word in the box. Write it on the line.**

dish	door	luck
ring	ship	mop

1. stop _____

2. sing _____

3. floor _____

4. fish _____

5. trip _____

6. truck _____

■ **Finish each question. Use a rhyming word from the box.**

way	bake	mess	pail
cash	pest	cone	tar

1. Have you ever found your mail thrown in a _____ ?

2. Have you ever made a cake that just wouldn't _____ ?

3. Have you ever seen a car that was made out of _____ ?

4. Did you ever get a rash from having too much _____ ?

5. Did you ever have a day when things went your _____ ?

6. Did you ever have a guest that became a real _____ ?

7. Did you ever own a phone that was shaped like a _____ ?

8. Did you ever try to guess who made a huge _____ ?

■ Words that mean almost the same thing are called **synonyms**.
   EXAMPLES:

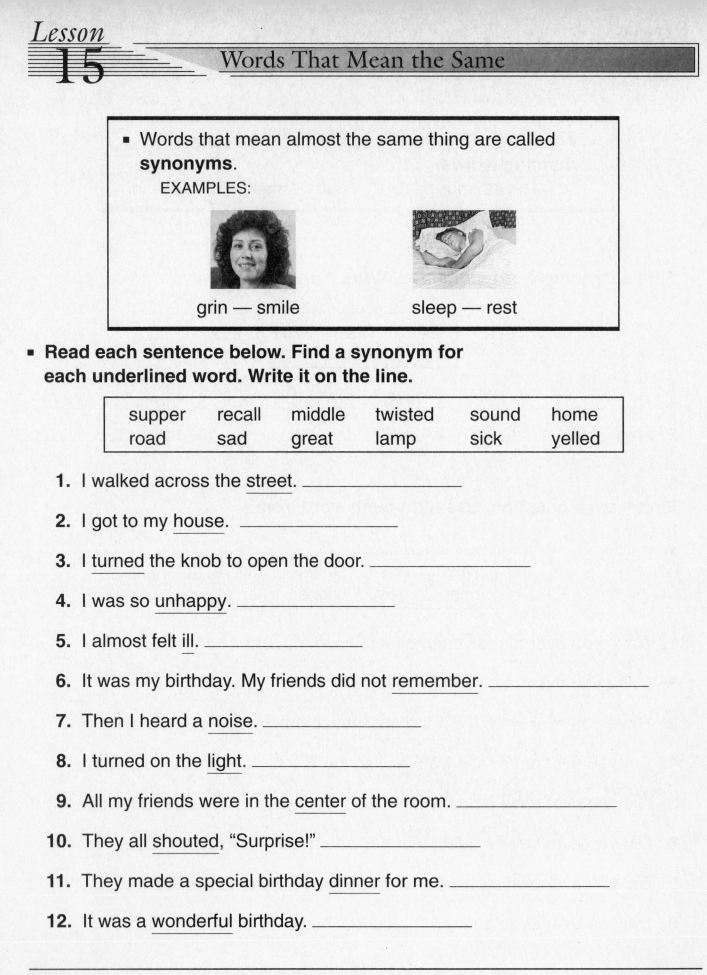

grin — smile   sleep — rest

■ **Read each sentence below. Find a synonym for each underlined word. Write it on the line.**

supper	recall	middle	twisted	sound	home
road	sad	great	lamp	sick	yelled

1. I walked across the street. _____

2. I got to my house. _____

3. I turned the knob to open the door. _____

4. I was so unhappy. _____

5. I almost felt ill. _____

6. It was my birthday. My friends did not remember. _____

7. Then I heard a noise. _____

8. I turned on the light. _____

9. All my friends were in the center of the room. _____

10. They all shouted, "Surprise!" _____

11. They made a special birthday dinner for me. _____

12. It was a wonderful birthday. _____

- Words that mean the opposite are called **antonyms**.
  EXAMPLES:

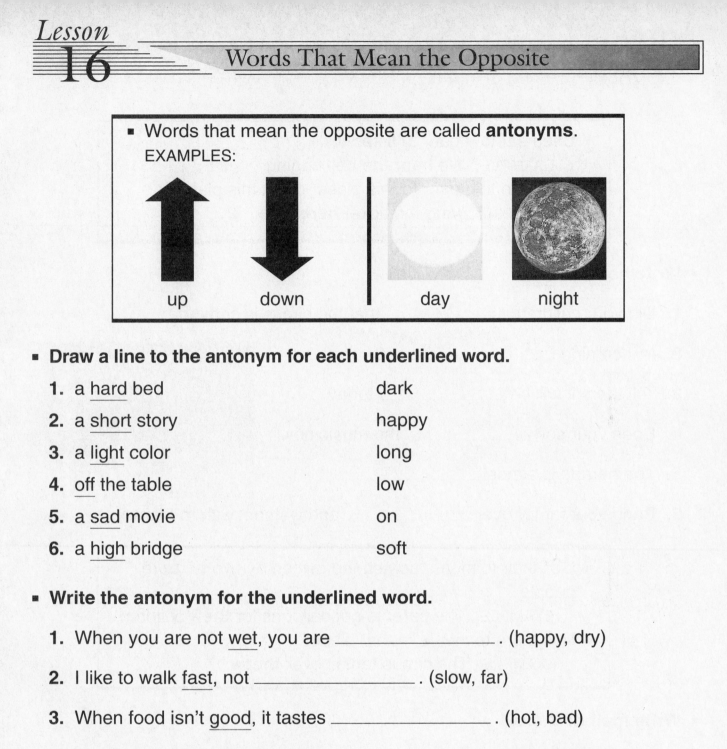

up　　　down　　　day　　　night

- **Draw a line to the antonym for each underlined word.**

  1. a <u>hard</u> bed　　　　　　　dark

  2. a <u>short</u> story　　　　　　happy

  3. a <u>light</u> color　　　　　　long

  4. <u>off</u> the table　　　　　　low

  5. a <u>sad</u> movie　　　　　　on

  6. a <u>high</u> bridge　　　　　soft

- **Write the antonym for the underlined word.**

  1. When you are not <u>wet</u>, you are _____ . (happy, dry)

  2. I like to walk <u>fast</u>, not _____ . (slow, far)

  3. When food isn't <u>good</u>, it tastes _____ . (hot, bad)

  4. Summer is <u>hot</u>, and winter is _____ . (cold, snow)

  5. A traffic light turns red for <u>stop</u> and green for _____ . (high, go)

  6. Some questions are <u>easy</u>. Others are _____ . (not, hard)

  7. My shoes were <u>clean</u>. Then they got _____ . (dirty, old)

  8. My boss will answer <u>yes</u> or _____ . (maybe, no)

> - Use <u>hear</u> to mean "to listen to."
>   EXAMPLE: We **hear** the bell ringing.
> - Use <u>here</u> to mean "to this place" or "at this place."
>   EXAMPLE: Bring the ticket **here**.

- **Write <u>hear</u> or <u>here</u>.**

1. Did your children _____ that the circus is coming?

2. Is it coming _____ soon?

3. Tell them it will be _____ today.

4. Does your son _____ the music now?

5. The parade is almost _____ .

6. Bring your family over _____ and watch it with my family.

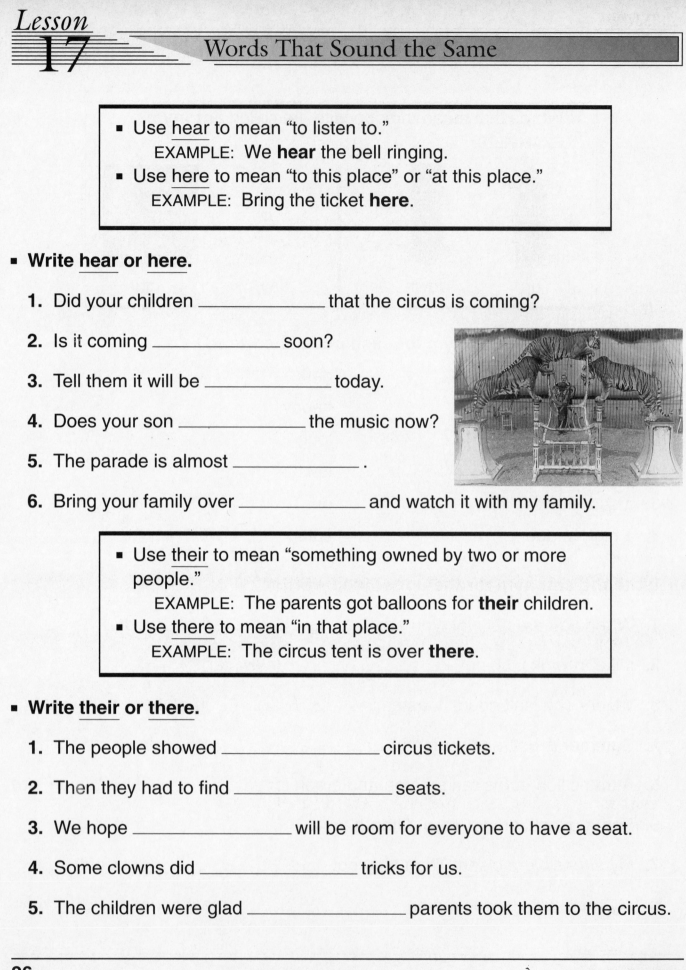

> - Use <u>their</u> to mean "something owned by two or more people."
>   EXAMPLE: The parents got balloons for **their** children.
> - Use <u>there</u> to mean "in that place."
>   EXAMPLE: The circus tent is over **there**.

- **Write <u>their</u> or <u>there</u>.**

1. The people showed _____ circus tickets.

2. Then they had to find _____ seats.

3. We hope _____ will be room for everyone to have a seat.

4. Some clowns did _____ tricks for us.

5. The children were glad _____ parents took them to the circus.

More Words That Sound the Same

- Use <u>write</u> to mean "to put words on paper."
  EXAMPLE: Please **write** your name on your paper.
- Use <u>right</u> to mean "correct."
  EXAMPLE: Your answer is **right**.
- Use <u>right</u> to mean "the opposite of left."
  EXAMPLE: Turn **right** to get to the bank.

- **Write <u>right</u> or <u>write</u>.**

  1. Chris likes to _____ letters to his friends.

  2. Martha knew her boss was _____ .

  3. We turn _____ to go to the store.

  4. Some people like to _____ stories.

  5. Kim parts her hair on the _____ side.

  6. Did you _____ a letter to your sister?

  7. Luis can _____ in Spanish.

  8. The teacher marked the _____ answers.

  9. Be sure you park in the _____ place.

  10. Jenna will _____ about her birthday party.

  11. James writes with his _____ hand.

- **Write two sentences about work. Use <u>write</u> in one sentence. Use <u>right</u> in the other sentence.**

  1. _____

  2. _____

> - Use <u>two</u> to mean "the number 2."
>   EXAMPLE: **Two** women worked together.
> - Use <u>too</u> to mean "more than enough."
>   EXAMPLE: There are **too** many people on the bus.
> - Use <u>too</u> to mean "also."
>   EXAMPLE: May I help, **too**?
> - Use <u>to</u> to mean "toward" or "to do something."
>   EXAMPLE: Let's go **to** the library **to** find Kim.

- **Write two, too, or to.**

1. Mr. and Mrs. Diaz walked _____ the store.

2. Mr. Diaz picked out _____ melons.

3. He handed them _____ his wife.

4. Then Mr. and Mrs. Diaz went _____ look at the frozen foods.

5. They needed _____ get some frozen peas.

6. "Do we need some frozen corn, _____?" asked Mr. Diaz.

7. "No, we have _____ much corn already," said Mrs. Diaz.

8. Mr. Diaz got _____ frozen dinners.

9. Then Mr. and Mrs. Diaz turned _____ the right.

10. They put _____ more things in the basket.

11. Mr. and Mrs. Diaz took their groceries _____ the clerk.

12. They gave money _____ the clerk for the groceries.

13. One grocery bag was _____ heavy.

14. Mr. Diaz asked the clerk _____ help him carry it.

- Some words have two different meanings.
  EXAMPLE: <u>Ring</u> means "something worn on the finger." Anna let me try on her **ring**. <u>Ring</u> also means "send out a clear sound." Did you hear the bell **ring**?

- **Look at each pair of photos. Read each sentence. Then write the letter of the correct meaning on the line.**

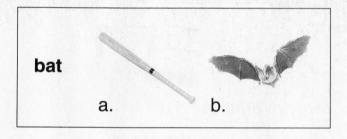

bat

a.   b.

plant

a.   b.

1. _____ Tony has a wooden bat.

2. _____ The bat sleeps during the day.

3. _____ The bat broke when Alberto hit the ball.

4. _____ Kendra wants to plant a vegetable garden.

5. _____ The farmer will plant his crops in the fall.

6. _____ This is a beautiful plant!

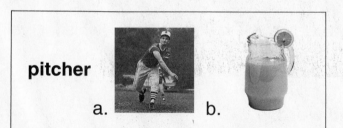

pitcher

a.   b.

wave

a.   b.

7. _____ The pitcher threw the ball.

8. _____ I put juice in the pitcher.

9. _____ The pitcher was empty.

10. _____ My baby can wave to people.

11. _____ An ocean wave is strong.

12. _____ The surfer rode a big wave.

- **Draw lines between the words that rhyme.**

  1. horn   fed

  2. sat   like

  3. hike   net

  4. shed   corn

  5. get   mat

- **Read the words. Write S if the underlined words are synonyms. Write A if they are antonyms.**

  _____ **1.** big car, small car   _____ **5.** over a house, under a house

  _____ **2.** first day, last day   _____ **6.** hot drink, cold drink

  _____ **3.** jump over, hop over   _____ **7.** old hat, new hat

  _____ **4.** large man, huge man   _____ **8.** feel happy, feel glad

- **Write the synonym for the underlined word.**

  1. A street is the same as a _____ . (road, gift)

  2. Something that is little is also _____ . (small, large)

  3. If you shout at someone, you _____ at that person. (whisper, yell)

  4. If you feel glad, you are _____ . (sad, happy)

- **Write the antonym for the underlined word.**

  1. If your hair is not wet, it is _____ . (damp, dry)

  2. When the work is not hard, it is _____ . (easy, difficult)

  3. A grapefruit can be sweet or _____ . (soft, sour)

  4. If you do not feel sad, you feel _____ . (happy, cold)

- **Write the correct word on the line.**

1. My neighbors cut _____ grass.
   (their, there)

2. Use your ears to _____ .
   (hear, here)

3. Juan said, "The twins are _____ ."
   (hear, here)

4. Did you _____ the good news?
   (hear, here)

5. Mrs. Sampson put the book _____ .
   (their, there)

6. David wants a pay raise, _____ .
   (to, too, two)

7. Linda went _____ see her friends in Calgary, Alberta.
   (to, too, two)

8. Anthony will _____ his name on the folder.
   (right, write)

9. Seth found _____ bills he forgot to pay.
   (to, too, two)

- **Look at the pair of photos. Read each sentence. Write the letter of the correct meaning on the line.**

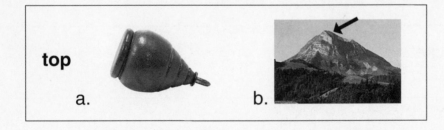

top

a.   b.

_____ 1. Frank taught his son how to spin a top.

_____ 2. The dog ran to the top of the stairs.

_____ 3. I put the book on the top shelf.

_____ 4. Sharita bought her daughter a top at the toy store.

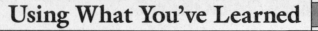

- **Read about Melissa's birthday present.**

> It is Melissa's birthday. Her husband hides a present. He writes clues to help Melissa find the present. The clues have antonyms in them.
>
> One sentence says, "Look <u>over</u> the desk." Then Melissa must look <u>under</u> the desk.

- **Now read the sentences Melissa's husband wrote. Write what Melissa must do.**

1. Walk <u>down</u> the stairs.

   <u>Walk up the stairs.</u>

2. Take two <u>small</u> steps.

   _____

3. <u>Close</u> the door.

   _____

4. Turn <u>off</u> the light.

   _____

5. Find the <u>old</u> shirt.

   _____

6. Find a <u>big</u> box in the pocket.

   _____

- **Answer the questions.**

1. What do you think Melissa found in the box?

   _____

2. What would you like to find in a small box?

   _____

- Randy took a vacation. He wrote a letter to his friends.
  He made ten spelling mistakes. Try to fix Randy's letter.
  Draw a line under the mistakes.

July 5, 1994

Dear Rosa and Marcos,

    <u>Hear</u> I am in Florida. I wanted too right you a letter
two tell you about my trip.

    Their are many interesting things too do and see
while I am hear. The thing I like best is going two here
different bands play each night.

    I'll see you in too weeks.

                Sincerely,

                Randy

- Write Randy's letter as it should be.

July 5, 1994

Dear Rosa and Marcos,

    Here I am _____

_____

_____

_____

_____

_____

                Sincerely,

                Randy

> - A **sentence** is a group of words that tells or asks something. It stands for a complete thought.
>   EXAMPLES: Friends talk. Cars go fast.

- **Write <u>yes</u> if the group of words is a sentence.**
  Write <u>no</u> if the group of words is not a sentence.

1. _____no_____ A long time ago.

2. _____ Our family went to the park.

3. _____ Near the tree.

4. _____ Ten squirrels played.

5. _____ Mark threw the ball to his dog.

6. _____ His dog chased the ball.

7. _____ Bill and Tom.

8. _____ Fished and relaxed all day.

9. _____ Everyone had fun.

10. _____ Jan lost a new ring.

11. _____ We ate lunch.

12. _____ Too hot for us.

13. _____ Our family talked about the picnic.

14. _____ Some people.

15. _____ Sang songs.

16. _____ Then we went home.

- **Draw lines between the groups of words to make sentences. Then read the sentences.**

    1. Mrs. Brown   live in our building.

    2. Our building   is made of wood.

    3. Four families   lives on my street.

    4. Our company   tasted great.

    5. The food   had a picnic.

    6. The sun   shone all day.

    7. Corn and beans   fed the baby goat.

    8. The wagon   has a broken wheel.

    9. The mother goat   grow on a farm.

    10. The boat   sailed in strong winds.

    11. The fisher   were sold in the store.

    12. Some of the fish   caught seven fish.

    13. Our team   hit the ball a lot.

    14. Our batters   won ten games.

    15. The ballpark   was full of fans.

- **Write a sentence about your job.**

    _____

    _____

- **Write a sentence about your house or apartment.**

    _____

    _____

- Words in a sentence must be in an order that makes sense.

   EXAMPLES: Mr. Danson plays baseball.
   My son writes stories.

- **Write these words in an order that makes sense.**

   1. friend My apples eats

   <u>My friend eats apples.</u>

   2. drinks Elizabeth milk

   _____

   3. to swim Kim likes

   _____

   4. Justin bread wants

   _____

   5. corn plants Ms. Carter

   _____

   6. a fish Chang caught

   _____

   7. breakfast cooks Shawn

   _____

   8. his shares Hoan lunch

   _____

   9. the Rosa planted tree

   _____

   10. the looks at Kate pie

   _____

- A **telling sentence** is a group of words that tells something.
  EXAMPLES: I fed my children. The children like to run and play.

- **Write telling on the line before the group of words if it is a telling sentence. Leave the line blank if it is not a sentence.**

_____telling_____ 1. Josh loves his new truck.

_____ 2. He got it yesterday.

_____ 3. Wide tires.

_____ 4. It can carry a heavy load.

_____ 5. It runs on natural gas.

_____ 6. Over the hills.

_____ 7. Josh enjoys driving the truck.

_____ 8. The truck is wide.

_____ 9. Down the highway.

_____ 10. Josh works hard.

_____ 11. After work.

_____ 12. Josh can work on the engine.

_____ 13. In the garage.

_____ 14. Josh washes the truck.

_____ 15. He keeps the truck clean.

> ▪ An **asking sentence** is a group of words that asks a question. You can answer an asking sentence.
>   EXAMPLES: How are you feeling? Where do you live?

▪ **Write asking on the line before the group of words if it is an asking sentence. Leave the line blank if the group of words is not a sentence.**

asking   **1.** Is this your friend?

_____ **2.** Where does she live?

_____ **3.** She is town?

_____ **4.** How was work today?

_____ **5.** Type and answer phones?

_____ **6.** What is on TV?

_____ **7.** Where is the newspaper?

_____ **8.** Look in the?

_____ **9.** When does the party begin?

_____ **10.** Do you have any chips?

_____ **11.** Where can we work on this?

_____ **12.** The kitchen in?

_____ **13.** Can you drive a car?

_____ **14.** Yes, I?

_____ **15.** Why did Sarah leave?

- **Write telling for telling sentences. Write asking for asking sentences.**

_____ **1.** Ms. Lopez went to the store.

_____ **2.** Where is the store?

_____ **3.** It is close to her house.

_____ **4.** What did she buy at the store?

_____ **5.** Ms. Lopez bought some food for dinner.

_____ **6.** She plans to make some stew.

_____ **7.** Did she buy potatoes?

_____ **8.** No, Ms. Lopez already had potatoes.

_____ **9.** Why did she check her list?

_____ **10.** She wants to be sure she didn't forget anything.

- **Read the sentences. Write each sentence under the correct heading.**

I went to the store.   Are there any vegetables?
What did you buy?   I bought some carrots.

Telling Sentences

_____

_____

Asking Sentences

_____

_____

> ▪ The naming part of a sentence tells who or what the sentence is about.
>
> EXAMPLES: **Three people** asked about the new job.
> **The boss** will hire one of them.

▪ **Circle the naming part of each sentence.**

1. (My family and I) live on a busy street.

2. Sally Harper goes to vote.

3. Miss Jenkins drives very slowly.

4. Mr. and Mrs. Avalos walk their dog.

5. Henry swings his racket.

6. Mr. Byrne cuts his grass.

7. Mrs. Lee picks up her children.

8. Dr. Diaz shops for food.

9. Jeanine walks in the park.

10. Mr. Wolf brings the mail.

11. Sam Taft reads the newspaper.

12. Ms. O'Dowd cooks dinner.

13. Nina paints the house.

14. Some families plant a garden.

15. Mrs. Clark washes her windows.

16. Carolyn and Albert plant flower seeds.

17. Julie waters the garden.

> - The action part of a sentence tells what someone or something does.
>   EXAMPLES: Three people **asked about the new job**.
>   The boss **will hire one of them**.

- **Circle the action part of each sentence.**

1. My family and I (live on a busy street.)

2. Sally Harper goes to vote.

3. Miss Jenkins drives very slowly.

4. Mr. and Mrs. Avalos walk their dog.

5. Henry swings his racket.

6. Mr. Byrne cuts his grass.

7. Mrs. Lee picks up her children.

8. Dr. Diaz shops for food.

9. Jeanine walks in the park.

10. Mr. Wolf brings the mail.

11. Sam Taft reads the newspaper.

12. Ms. O'Dowd cooks dinner.

13. Nina paints the house.

14. Some families plant a garden.

15. Mrs. Clark washes her windows.

16. Carolyn and Albert plant flower seeds.

17. Julie waters the garden.

- **Choose a naming part to complete each sentence.**

| Books | A pen | A hammer | Dinner | The watch | Music | My telephone |

1. ___Books___ are placed on shelves in the library.

2. _____ plays on the radio.

3. _____ hits the nail.

4. _____ uses ink.

5. _____ needs to be set to the correct time.

6. _____ rings until I pick it up.

7. _____ cooks on the stove.

- **Choose an action part to complete each sentence.**

| rings | stalls | reflects | ticks | bakes | shines | overflows |

1. The turkey in the oven ___bakes___ .

2. My doorbell _____ .

3. The water in the sink _____ .

4. His car engine _____ .

5. The clock _____ .

6. A mirror _____ .

7. The sun _____ .

- **Write a sentence about something that you like. Circle the naming part. Underline the action part.**

_____

- **Write S if the group of words is a sentence.**
  Write N if the group of words is not a sentence.

  _____ **1.** A job is.

  _____ **2.** Some people work with computers.

  _____ **3.** Office workers answer the phones.

  _____ **4.** Work outside.

- **Draw lines between the groups of words to make sentences.**

  1. Alan and Ellen   teaches them how to play.

  2. The big game   is Saturday night.

  3. Their coach   play on the same team.

  4. The phone   is calling from Toronto.

  5. Our friend   rush to answer it.

  6. Betty and Tom   rings.

  7. The hungry frog   ate an insect.

  8. Twenty geese   curled up to sleep.

  9. A cat   flew south for the winter.

- **Write the words in an order that makes sense.**

  1. Tom a good friend is

  _____

  2. next He door lives

  _____

  3. together to work We drive

  _____

- Write <u>telling</u> for a telling sentence.
  Write <u>asking</u> for an asking sentence.
  Leave the line blank if the group of words is not a sentence.

1. _____ Did you go to the store?

2. _____ What did you buy?

3. _____ I will buy a card for my husband.

4. _____ A present for my friend.

5. _____ Some eggs for breakfast.

6. _____ Ellen needs some rice.

7. _____ The baby wants some milk.

8. _____ Where is the fish?

9. _____ In the meat section.

10. _____ I hope I can carry everything.

11. _____ A large bag.

12. _____ Did I remember everything?

- Complete the sentences. Choose the naming part or the action part that is needed.

Many people go to a restaurant	Amanda tries something new

1. _____ go out to eat after work.

2. Amanda and Jeff _____.

3. _____ orders her favorite meal.

4. Jeff _____.

■ **Read the paragraph. Then read the pairs of sentences. Circle each asking sentence. Copy each asking sentence.**

Suki and Juan are students. They are learning about airplanes. Some day they might want to work for an airline. Suki asks Juan some questions about airplanes.

1. Would you like to work on an airplane?

   I would like to fly an airplane.

   _____

2. I flew to Ontario.

   Have you ever flown on an airplane?

   _____

3. How was the food on the airplane?

   The food tasted good.

   _____

4. My cousin flew in an airplane to visit me.

   Did your cousin enjoy the flight?

   _____

5. How do you get a job with an airline?

   You must apply at the airport.

   _____

6. I will go to the airport and fill out a form.

   May I go with you?

   _____

- **Make sentences that tell what Suki and Juan learned about airplanes. Draw a line from a naming part to an action part. Be sure the sentences make sense.**

Naming Part	Action Part
1. A big airport	are very big.
2. Many airplanes	flies the airplane.
3. The people on airplanes	is a busy place.
4. A pilot	wear seat belts.
5. Many airport workers	work very hard.

- **Write sentences by putting the words in an order that makes sense.**

1. friend The pilot is my

_____

2. flies She around the world

_____

3. countries many She sees

_____

4. I pilot's seat sat in the

_____

5. very big The is airport

_____

6. easy to get It is lost

_____

7. to fly I like would

_____

> • A **noun** is a word that names a person, place, or thing. The words a, an, and the are clues that show a noun is near.
>
> EXAMPLES: a **man**, the **yard**, an **elbow**

• **Find the nouns, or naming words, below. Write the nouns on the lines.**

apple	car	eat	hot	tree
bird	chair	gone	over	truck
box	desk	grass	pen	up
came	dirty	hear	rug	woman

1. _apple_

2. _____

3. _____

4. _____

5. _____

6. _____

7. _____

8. _____

9. _____

10. _____

11. _____

12. _____

• **Draw lines under the two nouns in each sentence. Write the nouns on the lines.**

1. The cook boiled an egg. _____ _____

2. A bird flies to the tree. _____ _____

3. A chair is by the desk. _____ _____

4. A man sits in the chair. _____ _____

5. The woman drives a truck. _____ _____

6. The truck is on the highway. _____ _____

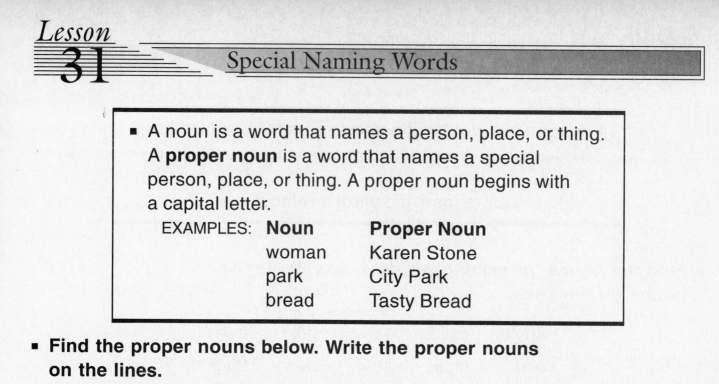

- A noun is a word that names a person, place, or thing. A **proper noun** is a word that names a special person, place, or thing. A proper noun begins with a capital letter.

EXAMPLES:

Noun	Proper Noun
woman	Karen Stone
park	City Park
bread	Tasty Bread

- **Find the proper nouns below. Write the proper nouns on the lines.**

baseball	China	man	prince
Bob's Bakery	Elf Corn	New York City	robin
Bridge Road	Gabriel	Ohio	State Street
parents	Ms. Valdez	Pat Green	village

1. _Bob's Bakery_

2. _____

3. _____

4. _____

5. _____

6. _____

7. _____

8. _____

9. _____

10. _____

- **Draw a line under the proper noun in each sentence. Write each proper noun on the line.**

1. I bought apples at Hill's Store. _____

2. The store is on Baker Street. _____

3. It is near Stone Library. _____

4. I gave an umbrella to Emily Fuller. _____

- **Draw a line under the two nouns, or naming words, in each sentence.**

    1. The <u>clerk</u> works at the <u>store</u>.

    2. Use the scale to weigh the vegetables.

    3. The shelves are full of food.

    4. Put the groceries in the sack.

- **Draw a line under the verb, or action word, in each sentence.**

    1. Mario <u>takes</u> his car to the car wash.

    2. He puts water on the car.

    3. Rosa pours soap all over the car.

    4. Juan rubs wax on the outside of the car.

    5. Then Mario vacuums the inside of the car.

- **Read the sentences. Write <u>noun</u> or <u>verb</u> for each underlined word.**

    1. The wind <u>blows</u> hard today. _____

    2. <u>Ed</u> and Susan fly their plane. _____

    3. Ed and Susan are <u>pilots</u>. _____

    4. The plane <u>climbs</u> into the sky. _____

    5. Suddenly one <u>engine</u> stops. _____

    6. <u>Susan</u> fixes the problem. _____

    7. Ed <u>smiles</u>. _____

    8. Ed and Susan enjoy the rest of the <u>flight</u>. _____

    9. The plane <u>lands</u> safely. _____

Adding *-ed* or *-ing* to Verbs

- To show that something happened in the past, add
  -ed to most verbs.
     EXAMPLE: Don **visited** Lita yesterday.
- To show that something is happening now, you can
  add -ing to most verbs.
     EXAMPLE: Sue is **visiting** Lita now.

- **Draw a line under the correct verb.**

  1. Terry and Joe (bowled, bowling) last week.

  2. Jenny (called, calling) them on the phone.

  3. She (wanted, wanting) to go bowling with them.

  4. The men are (invited, inviting) her to go on Saturday.

  5. Jenny (jumped, jumping) at the chance to go.

  6. She (scored, scoring) several strikes.

  7. Joe and Terry are (clapped, clapping) for Jenny.

  8. Now Jenny is (asked, asking) if she can be on their team.

  9. Joe and Terry are (smiled, smiling) at Jenny.

  10. Jenny (thanked, thanking) Terry and Joe.

- **Add -ed or -ing to each verb. Then
  rewrite each sentence.**

  1. Carmen is finish _____ her work now. _____

  _____

  2. Carmen help _____ her husband cook yesterday. _____

  _____

  3. Manuel is cook _____ some soup today. _____

  _____

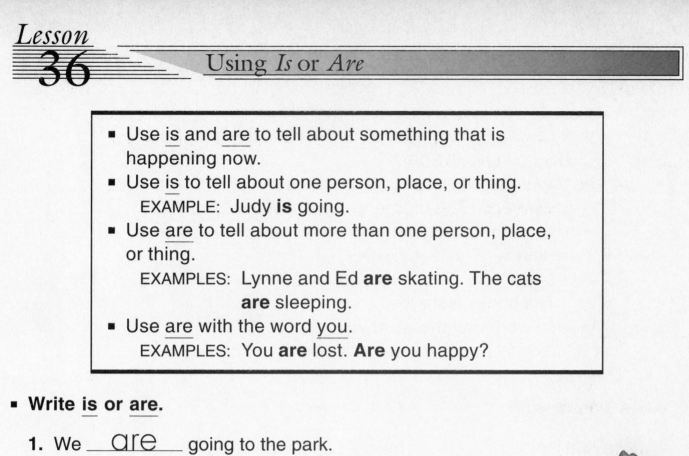

- Use <u>is</u> and <u>are</u> to tell about something that is happening now.
- Use <u>is</u> to tell about one person, place, or thing.
  EXAMPLE: Judy **is** going.
- Use <u>are</u> to tell about more than one person, place, or thing.
  EXAMPLES: Lynne and Ed **are** skating. The cats **are** sleeping.
- Use <u>are</u> with the word <u>you</u>.
  EXAMPLES: You **are** lost. **Are** you happy?

- **Write <u>is</u> or <u>are</u>.**

  1. We _____are_____ going to the park.

  2. Alan _____ going, too.

  3. Kate and Calvin _____ walking on the trail.

  4. Kate _____ faster than Calvin.

  5. Alan _____ getting a drink at the water fountain.

  6. Where _____ the water fountain?

  7. Those people _____ standing by the fountain.

  8. Kate _____ standing by the roses.

  9. The roses _____ lovely.

One rose is blooming.

Many roses are blooming.

- **Write one sentence about a park using <u>is</u>.**
  Write one sentence about a park using <u>are</u>.

  1. (is) _____

  2. (are) _____

> - Use <u>was</u> and <u>were</u> to tell about something that happened in the past.
> - Use <u>was</u> to tell about one person, place, or thing.
>   EXAMPLE: The broom **was** in the closet.
> - Use <u>were</u> to tell about more than one person, place, or thing.
>   EXAMPLES: Ten people **were** there.
>   The books **were** lost.
> - Use <u>were</u> with the word <u>you</u>.
>   EXAMPLES: You **were** late. **Were** you home?

- **Write <u>was</u> or <u>were</u>.**

1. Sara and Bill _____ excited about their new house.

2. I _____ showing them around the house.

3. The workers _____ indoors while it rained.

4. José _____ putting up the wallpaper.

5. Scott and Jay _____ painting the kitchen.

6. Ann, Roy, and Jamie _____ laying the carpet.

7. Nick _____ connecting the washer and dryer.

8. You _____ waiting to deliver the furniture.

9. Steve _____ taking a break.

- **Write one sentence about a rainy day using <u>was</u>.**
  Write one sentence about a rainy day using <u>were</u>.

1. (was) _____

2. (were) _____

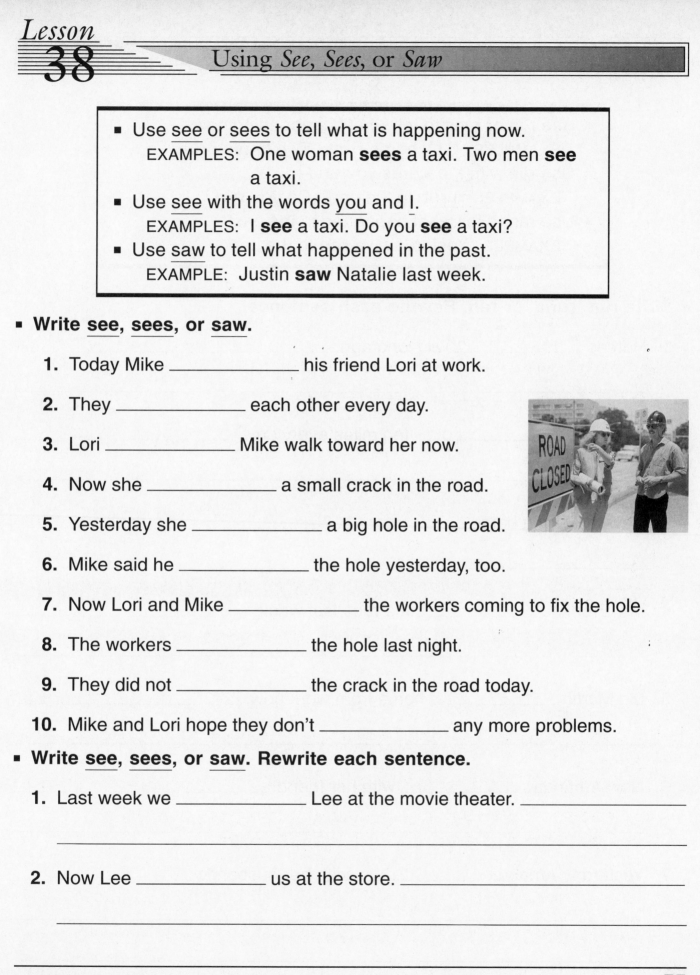

> - Use <u>see</u> or <u>sees</u> to tell what is happening now.
>   EXAMPLES: One woman **sees** a taxi. Two men **see** a taxi.
> - Use <u>see</u> with the words <u>you</u> and <u>I</u>.
>   EXAMPLES: I **see** a taxi. Do you **see** a taxi?
> - Use <u>saw</u> to tell what happened in the past.
>   EXAMPLE: Justin **saw** Natalie last week.

- **Write <u>see</u>, <u>sees</u>, or <u>saw</u>.**

1. Today Mike _____ his friend Lori at work.

2. They _____ each other every day.

3. Lori _____ Mike walk toward her now.

4. Now she _____ a small crack in the road.

5. Yesterday she _____ a big hole in the road.

6. Mike said he _____ the hole yesterday, too.

7. Now Lori and Mike _____ the workers coming to fix the hole.

8. The workers _____ the hole last night.

9. They did not _____ the crack in the road today.

10. Mike and Lori hope they don't _____ any more problems.

- **Write <u>see</u>, <u>sees</u>, or <u>saw</u>. Rewrite each sentence.**

1. Last week we _____ Lee at the movie theater. _____

   _____

2. Now Lee _____ us at the store. _____

   _____

- Use <u>run</u> or <u>runs</u> to tell what is happening now.
  EXAMPLES: One horse **runs**. Two horses **run**.
- Use <u>run</u> with the words <u>you</u> and I.
  EXAMPLES: I **run** in the park. Do you **run**?
- Use <u>ran</u> to tell what happened in the past.
  EXAMPLE: Yesterday we **ran** to the park.

- **Write <u>run</u>, <u>runs</u>, or <u>ran</u>. Rewrite each sentence.**

1. Horses _____ wild long ago. _____

   _____

2. A horse can _____ ten miles every day. _____

   _____

3. How fast can a horse _____ ? _____

   _____

4. Ms. Brooks _____ in a race last week. _____

   _____

5. Mr. Martin _____ home from work now. _____

   _____

6. Now Amanda _____ with her friend. _____

   _____

7. Yesterday Amanda _____ with her husband. _____

   _____

> - Use <u>give</u> or <u>gives</u> to tell what is happening now.
>   EXAMPLES: One person **gives** a gift. Two people **give** a gift.
> - Use <u>give</u> with the words <u>you</u> and <u>I</u>.
>   EXAMPLES: I **give** a gift. Do you **give** one?
> - Use <u>gave</u> to tell what happened in the past.
>   EXAMPLE: Jeff **gave** me a present yesterday.

- **Write <u>give</u>, <u>gives</u>, or <u>gave</u>.**

  1. Juan _____ the chickens corn now.

  2. The chickens _____ us eggs to eat yesterday.

  3. Can you _____ the cow some hay?

  4. Sandra _____ the cow fresh water yesterday.

  5. Who _____ hay to the cow then?

  6. Our cow _____ us milk yesterday.

  7. We _____ the kittens some of the milk last night.

  8. I _____ food to the pigs last Monday.

  9. Mary _____ food to the sheep now.

  10. Our two sheep _____ us wool for warm coats.

- **Write three sentences about gifts using <u>give</u>, <u>gives</u>, and <u>gave</u>.**

  1. _____

  2. _____

  3. _____

■ Use does to tell about one person, place, or thing.
  EXAMPLE: William **does** the work.
■ Use do to tell about more than one person, place, or thing.
  EXAMPLE: They **do** the work.
■ Also use do with the words you and I.
  EXAMPLES: I **do** the work. You **do** the work.

■ **Write do or does.**

1. We _____ a great deal of work in the house.

2. My husband _____ all the dishes.

3. My nephew _____ the windows.

4. My daughter _____ the sweeping.

5. My niece _____ the sewing.

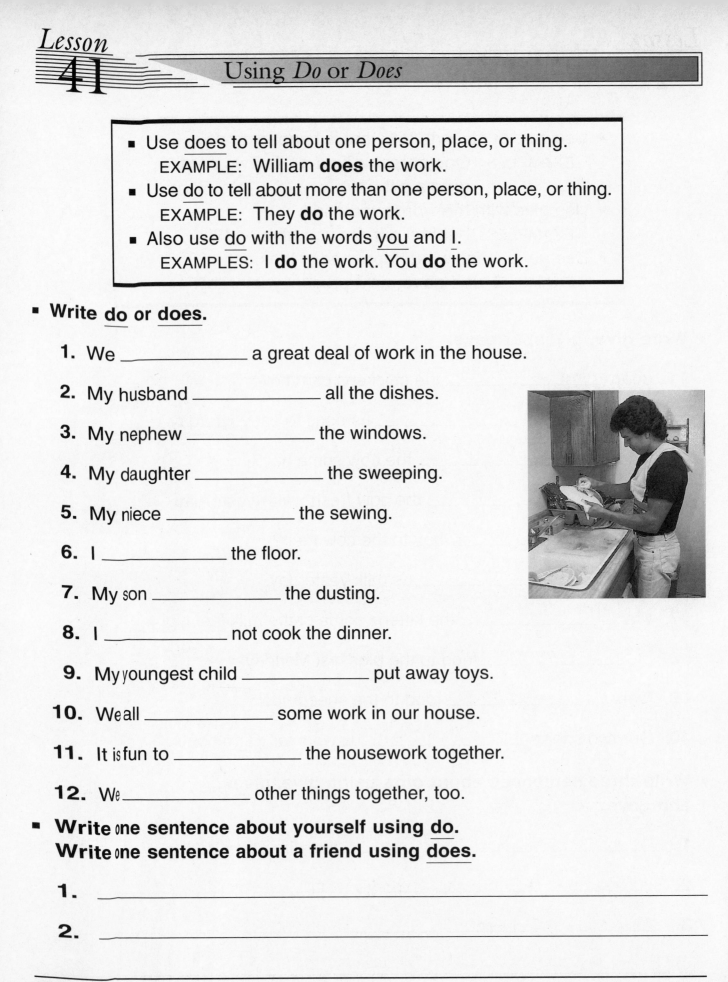

6. I _____ the floor.

7. My son _____ the dusting.

8. I _____ not cook the dinner.

9. My youngest child _____ put away toys.

10. We all _____ some work in our house.

11. It is fun to _____ the housework together.

12. We _____ other things together, too.

■ **Write one sentence about yourself using do.**
  Write one sentence about a friend using does.

1. _____

2. _____

- Use <u>has</u> to tell about one person, place, or thing.
  EXAMPLE: Jesse **has** a computer.
- Use <u>have</u> to tell about more than one person, place, or thing.
  EXAMPLE: Cars **have** tires.
- Use <u>have</u> with the words <u>you</u> and <u>I</u>.
  EXAMPLES: You **have** new shoes. I **have** a cold.
- Use <u>had</u> to tell about the past.
  EXAMPLES: My dogs **had** fleas. Bill **had** a pizza for dinner last night.

- **Write <u>has</u>, <u>have</u>, or <u>had</u>.**

1. Trina _____ the flu last week.

2. She _____ a fever last Monday.

3. Trina _____ to stay home from work when she was sick.

4. She _____ to stay in bed last Monday and Tuesday.

5. Now Trina's two children _____ the flu.

6. Trina _____ to take care of them now.

7. The children _____ a doctor's appointment in two hours.

8. Today Trina _____ borrowed a car to take the children to the doctor.

9. The doctor _____ many patients in the waiting room.

10. Most of the patients _____ the flu.

11. Last week the doctor _____ many flu patients, too.

12. The doctor _____ flu shots for people who aren't sick.

13. Trina and her children _____ flu shots last year.

> - A **pronoun** is a word that takes the place of a noun.
>   Some pronouns are <u>he</u>, <u>she</u>, <u>it</u>, <u>we</u>, <u>you</u>, <u>they</u>, and <u>I</u>.
>
>   EXAMPLE: Bill plays the guitar.   He plays the guitar.

- **Rewrite these sentences. Choose a pronoun to take the place of the words in the dark boxes.**

He	She	It	We	They

1. Alicia got a gift.

   She got a gift.

2. The gift was for her birthday.

   _____

3. Jamal brought the gift.

   _____

4. Kim and Tim went to Alicia's party.

   _____

5. Ellen and I are going to the party.

   _____

6. Rosa and Luis will bring a surprise.

   _____

7. Sue baked a cake for Alicia.

   _____

8. The party will end soon.

   _____

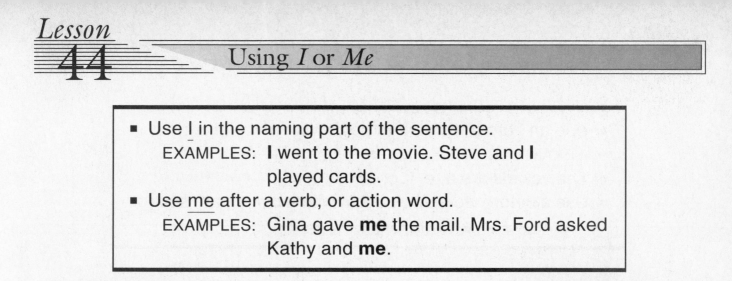

- Use I in the naming part of the sentence.
  EXAMPLES: **I** went to the movie. Steve and **I**
  played cards.
- Use me after a verb, or action word.
  EXAMPLES: Gina gave **me** the mail. Mrs. Ford asked
  Kathy and **me**.

- **Circle I or me.**

1. (I, Me) called Ms. Atkins for an interview.

2. Ms. Atkins asked (I, me) a few questions.

3. I told her Miss Long and (I, me) work well together.

4. She wants to interview Miss Long and (I, me).

5. Miss Long and (I, me) would like to work for Ms. Atkins.

6. (I, Me) hope Ms. Atkins will hire us.

- **Write I or me.**

1. _____ went to the clinic to get information.

2. My wife and _____ wanted to stop smoking.

3. The doctor said she could help my wife and _____ .

4. She asked _____ if we could come together.

5. _____ came for the appointment.

6. My wife met _____ there.

7. Each week the doctor talked to my wife and _____ .

8. _____ was glad when we finally quit smoking.

- Use <u>an</u> before words that begin with a vowel sound.
  EXAMPLES: **an** apple, **an** egg
- The vowels are <u>a</u>, <u>e</u>, <u>i</u>, <u>o</u>, and <u>u</u>.
- Use <u>a</u> before words that begin with a consonant sound.
  EXAMPLES: **a** car, **a** stove

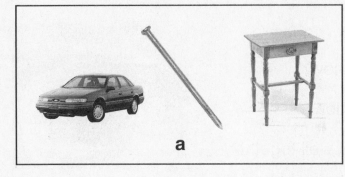

a

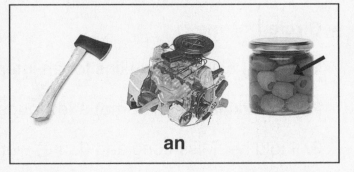

an

a car   a nail   a table   an ax   an engine   an olive

- **Write <u>a</u> or <u>an</u>.**

1. _____ arm
2. _____ dog
3. _____ hat
4. _____ ace
5. _____ cat
6. _____ exit
7. _____ ear

8. _____ office
9. _____ fire
10. _____ radio
11. _____ can
12. _____ tree
13. _____ inch
14. _____ oar

15. _____ key
16. _____ boat
17. _____ door
18. _____ oven
19. _____ eagle
20. _____ pet
21. _____ uncle

22. Randy ate _____ apple for lunch.

23. Victor likes fixing up _____ old building.

24. Linda bought two skirts and _____ shirt.

> - Add -er to most words to compare two people or two things.
>   EXAMPLE: Matt is tall. Clare is tall**er** than Matt.
> - Add -est to most words to compare more than two people or two things.
>   EXAMPLE: Cleo is the tall**est** person in the office.

■ **Add -er or -est. Write the sentences.**

1. Daryl is young _____ than Monica.

_____

2. Kim is the old _____ worker in the factory.

_____

3. A centimeter is small _____ than a meter.

_____

4. That trail is the long _____ one in the park.

_____

5. Our apartment is quiet _____ than your house.

_____

6. Mr. Mata is strong _____ than his son.

_____

7. That blue chair is the soft _____ in the room.

_____

- **Circle the two nouns in each sentence. Draw a line under the verb in each sentence.**

    1. The couple sat on the beach.

    2. The sand hurts their feet.

    3. Boats float on the waves.

- **Write each proper noun on the line.**

    1. Mr. Harper is my boss. _____

    2. My family lives in Colorado. _____

    3. Our house is on Tom Adams Drive. _____

    4. We live near Granger Park. _____

- **Add -s or -es to each word in ( ). Write the word on the line.**

    1. They wear _____ to work.
       (dress)

    2. The _____ hold many things.
       (box)

    3. Wildflowers grow under the _____ .
       (tree)

    4. We saw two _____ in the woods.
       (fox)

- **Draw a line under the correct verb.**

    1. José is (opened, opening) his present.

    2. He (pulled, pulling) the ribbon from the box.

    3. Janet was (played, playing) tennis.

    4. The dog (jumped, jumping) on the chair.

    5. The neighbors were (looked, looking) out their window.

- **Draw a line under the correct word.**

   1. Greg (is, are) working on his car.

   2. His friends (was, were) helping him.

   3. The car had (a, an) flat tire last week.

   4. Greg (has, have, had) a new tire today.

   5. Now the car (run, runs, ran) well.

   6. Greg (give, gives, gave) me another job yesterday.

   7. Greg told (I, me) to get the hammer.

   8. (I, Me) helped Greg fix the window.

   9. Then we shared (a, an) apple for a snack.

   10. It was the (bigger, biggest) apple I've ever seen.

- **Write see, saw, do, or does.**

   1. Now you can _____ my new car.

   2. I _____ your new car last night.

   3. Marla and I _____ many things to take care of it.

   4. But Marla _____ most of the work.

- **Rewrite these sentences. Use a pronoun from the box to take the place of the underlined words.**

   | He | She | It | We | They |

   1. Rosa and I went to a movie.

   _____

   2. Maria and Dave said it was a good movie.

   _____

   3. Maria wants to see it again.

   _____

- **Write the correct words on the lines.**

John: Jeff and _____ are twins.
(I, me)

Jeff: We _____ born on the same day.
(was, were)

John: I am _____ than Jeff.
(old, older)

I _____ born one minute before
(was, were)

Jeff. Our brother James is the

_____ of all the children.
(older, oldest)

Jeff: Our mother was surprised when she saw us.

_____ was not ready for two babies.
(She, He)

Our father was surprised when he _____
(see, saw)

two of us, too.

John: After we were born, our father _____ to
(ran, run)

the telephone.

Jeff: He _____ our grandmother.
(called, calling)

John: He said, " _____ you believe this?
(Do, Does)

Now we _____ two babies!"
(has, have)

- **Write the correct words on the lines.**

Yesterday _____ a special day for Robert. He
(was, were)

_____ a new job. His family _____ a big
(started, starting)   (had, have)

dinner to celebrate. They _____ very proud of him.
(was, were)

Everyone in the family helped _____ dinner
(gets, get)

ready. Robert said, "Maggie and _____ will set the
(me, I)

table." Tanya and Sharise _____ the food on the
(put, puts)

table. The family could _____ that it was quite
(see, saw)

a feast.

During dinner, Robert told how _____ got the
(he, she)

job. He said he filled out _____ application. His
(a, an)

application was _____ than any of the others. He
(neater, neatest)

had _____ interview. He wore the _____
(a, an)   (nicer, nicest)

suit he owned.

Robert _____ the woman who interviewed him.
(liked, liking)

The woman could tell Robert would _____ a great
(does, do)

job. She _____ him right away.
(hired, hiring)

Writing Names of People

> ■ Each word of a person's name begins with a **capital letter.**   EXAMPLE: **M**ary **A**nn **M**iller

■ **Rewrite the names. Use capital letters where they are needed.**

1. mark twain $\underline{\text{Mark Twain}}$

2. bill clinton _____

3. roy mayers _____

4. michael jordan _____

5. leslie ford _____

> ■ Each word of a family name begins with a capital letter.
> EXAMPLE: Here comes **A**unt **A**nn and **G**randpa.

■ **Circle the letters that should be capital letters.**

1. Today mother called grandma.

2. I will see grandma and grandpa at the party.

3. Will uncle carlos and aunt kathy be there, too?

■ **Rewrite the sentences. Use capital letters where they are needed.**

1. Did dad help mom?

_____

2. grandma and I made dinner.

_____

3. uncle frank is visiting us.

_____

Lesson
48

> ▪ An **initial** stands for a person's name. It is a capital letter with a **period** (.) after it.
>
> EXAMPLE: Steven Bell Mathis =
> Steven **B.** Mathis or **S. B.** Mathis or **S. B. M.**

▪ **Write the initials of each name.**

1. Robert Lawson R. L.

2. Carrie Anne Collier _____

3. Marcia Brown _____

4. Michael Bond _____

5. Carol Frank _____

6. Teresa Lynn Turner _____

7. Isaiah Bradley _____

8. Lou Ann Walker _____

▪ **Rewrite the names. Use initials for the names that are underlined.**

1. Joan Walsh Anglund

_____

2. Lee Bennett Hopkins

_____

3. Jane Yolen

_____

4. Patricia Ann Rosen

_____

▪ **Rewrite the sentences. Be sure to write the initials correctly.**

1. The box was for m s mills.

_____

2. d e ellis sent it to her.

_____

3. t j lee brought the box to the house.

_____

Writing Titles of Respect

- Begin a title of respect with a capital letter.
- End <u>Mr.</u>, <u>Mrs.</u>, <u>Ms.</u>, and <u>Dr.</u> with a period. They are short forms, or **abbreviations**, of longer words.
  EXAMPLES: **Mr.** George Selden   **Dr.** Alice Dahl
- Do not end <u>Miss</u> with a period.

- **Rewrite the names correctly.**

  1. mrs ruth scott _____

  2. mr kurt wiese _____

  3. miss e garcia _____

  4. dr washington _____

  5. ms carol baylor _____

  6. mr and mrs h cox _____

  7. miss k e jones _____

- **Rewrite the sentences correctly.**

  1. mrs h stone is here to see dr brooks.

  _____

  2. dr brooks and ms miller are not here.

  _____

  3. miss ari and mr lee came together.

  _____

  4. mr f green will go in first.

  _____

- Names of streets, parks, lakes, rivers, and schools begin with a capital letter.
  EXAMPLES: First Street
  Red River
  Central Park

- **Rewrite the sentences. Use capital letters where they are needed.**

1. James lives on market street.

_____

2. I think thomas park is in this town.

_____

3. We went to mathis lake for a picnic.

_____

4. Is seton school far away?

_____

- The abbreviations of the words <u>street</u>, <u>road</u>, and <u>drive</u> in a place name begin with a capital letter and end with a period.
  EXAMPLES: Street = **St.**   Main St.
  Road = **Rd.**   Dove Rd.   Drive = **Dr.**   East Dr.

- **Rewrite the place names. Use abbreviations.**

1. webb street _____   **4.** hill road _____

2. airport road _____   **5.** bell street _____

3. doe drive _____   **6.** oak drive _____

- Names of days of the week begin with a capital letter.
  EXAMPLES: **M**onday, **F**riday
- The abbreviations of days of the week begin with a capital letter. They end with a period.
  EXAMPLES: **S**un., **M**on., **T**ues., **W**ed., **T**hurs., **F**ri., **S**at.

Sunday	Monday	Tuesday	Wednesday	Thursday	Friday	Saturday
		1	2	3	4	5
6	7	8	9	10	11	12

- **Write the days to complete each sentence.**

1. The first of the week is _____ .

2. The day that comes before Saturday is _____ .

3. The day in the middle of the week is _____ .

4. Today is _____ .

5. I like _____ best.

- **Write the correct full name of each day. Then write the correct abbreviation.**

1. sunday _____ _____

2. monday _____ _____

3. tuesday _____ _____

4. wednesday _____ _____

5. thursday _____ _____

6. friday _____ _____

7. saturday _____ _____

> - Names of the months begin with a capital letter.
> - The abbreviations of the months begin with a capital letter. They end with a period.
>   EXAMPLES: **J**an., **F**eb., **M**ar., **D**ec.

- **Write the months of the year correctly.**

1. january   _____

2. february   _____

3. march   _____

4. april   _____

5. may   _____

6. june   _____

7. july   _____

8. august   _____

9. september _____

10. october   _____

11. november _____

12. december _____

- **Write the abbreviations of the months correctly.**

1. jan _____   4. aug _____   7. oct _____

2. mar _____   5. sept _____   8. dec _____

3. nov _____   6. feb _____   9. apr _____

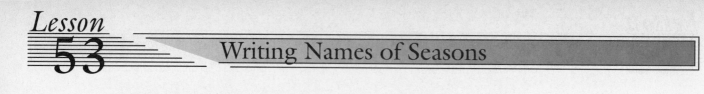

- Names of the four seasons do not begin with capital letters.

  EXAMPLES: **w**inter, **s**pring, **s**ummer, **f**all

winter	spring	summer	fall
December	March	June	September
January	April	July	October
February	May	August	November

- **Write the names of the four seasons on the top lines. Then list the months under the season.**

- **Complete each sentence with the name of a season.**

1. In _____ , we wear coats and gloves.

2. In _____ , trees turn green, and flowers grow.

3. In _____ , we swim outdoors.

4. In _____ , tree leaves turn red and yellow.

> - Each word in the name of a holiday begins with a capital letter.   EXAMPLES: **V**alentine's **D**ay
>   **M**emorial **D**ay

- **Write the holiday names correctly.**

1. new year's day _____

2. mother's day _____

3. independence day _____

4. labor day _____

5. victoria day _____

6. thanksgiving day _____

- **Rewrite each sentence correctly.**

1. January 1 is new year's day.

   _____

2. I like valentine's day.

   _____

3. boxing day is a British holiday.

   _____

4. father's day is in June.

   _____

5. thanksgiving is on Thursday.

   _____

6. We have a picnic on independence day.

   _____

> ■ The first and last words in a book title begin with a capital letter.
> ■ All other words begin with a capital letter except unimportant words. Some unimportant words are a, an, the, of, with, for, at, in, and on.
>
> EXAMPLES: The Earth and Beyond
> Working with Numbers

■ **Write these book titles correctly.**

1. the wonders of science

_____

2. protecting wildlife

_____

3. conserving the atmosphere

_____

4. mathematics in daily living

_____

5. reading for today

_____

6. great disasters

_____

7. choosing good health

_____

8. waste and recycling

_____

- Begin a sentence with a capital letter.
  EXAMPLE: **N**ow Deb and Tran work together.

- **Rewrite these sentences. Begin them with a capital letter.**

1. deb and Tran work for a book store.

   _____

2. tran answers the phone.

   _____

3. he takes the orders called in by customers.

   _____

4. deb types the orders into the computer.

   _____

5. she prints out a copy of each order.

   _____

6. then she gives the printouts to Tran.

   _____

7. tran looks at each printout.

   _____

8. the printouts show which books have been ordered.

   _____

9. tran packs each order into a box.

   _____

10. then Deb mails the boxes.

    _____

> ▪ Put a **period** (.) at the end of a sentence that tells something.   EXAMPLE: Patty is my friend.

▪ **Rewrite these telling sentences.
Use capital letters and periods.**

1. patty played on the softball team

_____

2. she played hard

_____

3. she hit two home runs

_____

> ▪ Put a **question mark** (**?**) at the end of a sentence that asks something.   EXAMPLE: Is he your brother?

▪ **Rewrite these asking sentences.
Use capital letters and question marks.**

1. what time is it

_____

2. is it time for lunch

_____

3. are you ready to eat

_____

4. would you like dessert

_____

> ■ A **comma** (,) may take the place of the word <u>and</u> if a sentence lists three or more things. Keep the last <u>and</u>.
>
> EXAMPLE: I bought paper **and** pens **and** pencils **and** staples for work.
> I bought paper, pens, pencils, **and** staples for work.

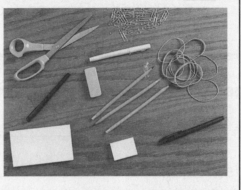

■ **Put commas where they are needed.**

1. I go to work on Monday Tuesday Wednesday Thursday and Friday.

2. I met with Jenna Charles and Ling on Monday.

3. After work I went to the store the post office and the dry cleaners.

4. My friend and I ate a pizza topped with mushrooms pepperoni and olives.

5. We saw Karen James and Janet at home.

■ **Rewrite the sentences. Use commas, and drop <u>and</u> where needed.**

1. Pam and Kay and Juan work hard.

_____

2. Pam sings and dances and acts in the play.

_____

3. Kay cleans and fixes and paints the stage.

_____

> ■ Names of cities and states begin with a capital letter.
> ■ Put a comma between the name of a city and its state.
>   EXAMPLES: Denver, Colorado
>   New York, New York

■ **Write the cities and states correctly.**

1. akron ohio _____

2. hilo hawaii _____

3. macon georgia _____

4. nome alaska _____

5. provo utah _____

■ **Rewrite the sentences. Use capital letters and commas where they are needed.**

1. Nancy lives in barnet vermont.

_____

2. Mr. Hill went to houston texas.

_____

3. Did Bruce like bend oregon?

_____

4. Will Amy visit macon missouri?

_____

5. How far away is salem maine?

_____

> ■ Put a comma between the day of the month and the year.   EXAMPLE: July 4, 1776

■ **Write these dates correctly. Use capital letters, periods, and commas where they are needed.**

1. dec 12 1948 _____

2. mar 27 1965 _____

3. sept 8 1994 _____

4. nov 1 1999 _____

5. jan 5 1995 _____

■ **Complete the sentences. Write the date correctly on the line.**

1. Jim was born on _____.
(august 10 1967)

2. Jen's birthday is _____.
(oct 17 1983)

3. Maria visited on _____.
(february 8 1991)

4. Dave's party was on _____.
(july 29 1993)

5. Carrie started work on _____.
(sept 3 1994)

6. My driver's license expires on _____.
(march 17 1996)

7. Luis bought his car on _____.
(oct 20 1992)

8. I was born on _____.

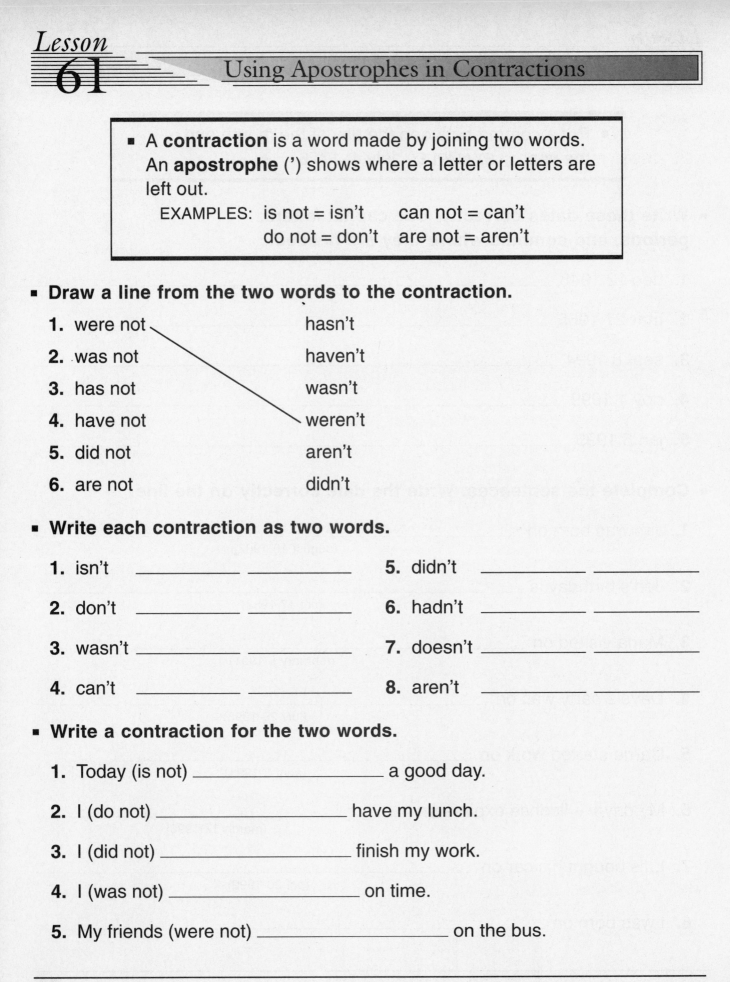

Lesson 61 — Using Apostrophes in Contractions

■ A **contraction** is a word made by joining two words.
An **apostrophe** (') shows where a letter or letters are left out.

EXAMPLES: is not = isn't   can not = can't
do not = don't   are not = aren't

■ **Draw a line from the two words to the contraction.**

1. were not   hasn't
2. was not   haven't
3. has not   wasn't
4. have not   weren't
5. did not   aren't
6. are not   didn't

■ **Write each contraction as two words.**

1. isn't _____ _____   5. didn't _____ _____
2. don't _____ _____   6. hadn't _____ _____
3. wasn't _____ _____   7. doesn't _____ _____
4. can't _____ _____   8. aren't _____ _____

■ **Write a contraction for the two words.**

1. Today (is not) _____ a good day.
2. I (do not) _____ have my lunch.
3. I (did not) _____ finish my work.
4. I (was not) _____ on time.
5. My friends (were not) _____ on the bus.

- **Circle the letters that should be capital letters.**

  1. grandpa has a turtle named speedy.

  2. our two cats are named brownie and mittens.

  3. dr. atwood has a fish named goldie.

  4. melissa and josé own a horse named sunny.

- **Write the sentences correctly.**

  1. mr w bell didnt work on friday

  _____

  2. june isnt a winter month

  _____

  3. is thanksgiving in november

  _____

  4. wasnt ms e smith planning the earth day activities

  _____

- **Rewrite the place names. Use abbreviations.**

  1. fifth street _____

  2. red river road _____

  3. adams drive _____

- **Write the correct abbreviation for each day.**

  1. Monday _____   4. Tuesday _____

  2. Wednesday _____   5. Friday _____

  3. Saturday _____   6. Thursday _____

- **Write these dates correctly.**

  1. july 4 1990 _____

  2. sept 5 1991 _____

  3. jan 20 1993 _____

  4. apr 1 1994 _____

- **Write these book titles correctly.**

  1. the joy of cooking _____

  2. jurassic park _____

- **Rewrite the sentences. Put commas where they are needed.**

  1. Trina jumped ran and swam to win first place.

  _____

  2. The seasons are winter spring summer and fall.

  _____

  3. Dionne lives in Seattle Washington.

  _____

  4. This letter is going to Chicago Illinois.

  _____

- **Write the contraction for the two words.**

  1. were not _____   **4.** do not _____

  2. has not _____   **5.** can not _____

  3. are not _____   **6.** is not _____

- **Everyone in Mr. Barton's family went on a trip. Imagine where and when each person might have gone. In the list below, draw a line from each person's name to the name of a place and then to a date. Then make a sentence about each person's trip. Be sure to use capital letters and punctuation correctly.**

1. grandpa barton	stone park	oct 12 1992
2. grandma barton	yellowstone park	july 24 1994
3. mr barton	sunny beach	june 14 1993
4. mrs barton	oak tree zoo	may 30 1994
5. becky barton	raceway rides	sept 2 1990
6. david barton	sea world	april 12 1993

1. Grandpa Barton went to Yellowstone Park on Sept. 2, 1990.

2. _____

3. _____

4. _____

5. _____

6. _____

■ Answer these questions about yourself.

1. What is your name?

   My name is _____.

2. What city and state do you live in?

   I live in _____.

3. Name the people in your family.

   The people in my family are _____.

4. Name two of your friends.

   My friends are _____.

5. What two holidays do you like best?

   I like _____.

6. What three months do you like best?

   I like _____.

7. What are four things you like to eat?

   I like to eat _____.

8. What are three things you like to do after work?

   After work I like to _____.

9. Where do you like to go on Saturdays?

   On Saturdays I like to go _____.

Writing Sentences

> - Remember that **sentences** have a naming part and an action part.
>   EXAMPLE: Sarah won the prize.

- **Draw a line from a naming part to an action part to make sentences.**

Naming Part	Action Part
1. The workers	reads.
2. Sue Miller	sings.
3. My friend	baked.
4. Sharise's son	eat.
5. Angela's husband	cooks.
6. Jon's wife	worked.

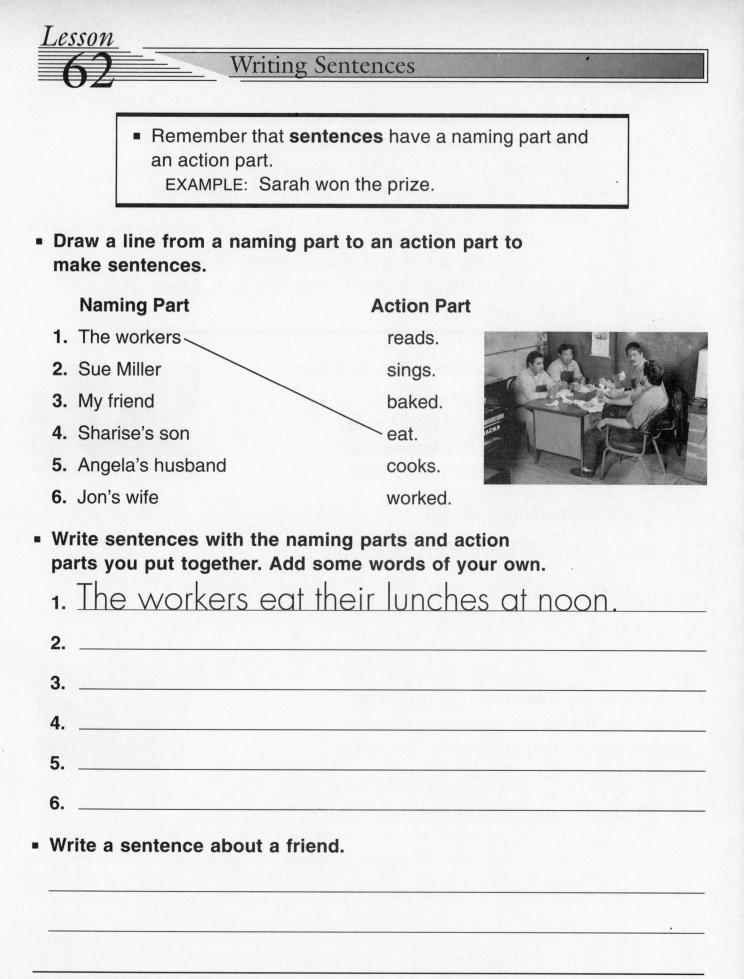

- **Write sentences with the naming parts and action parts you put together. Add some words of your own.**

1. The workers eat their lunches at noon.

2. _____

3. _____

4. _____

5. _____

6. _____

- **Write a sentence about a friend.**

_____

_____

- A **paragraph** is a group of sentences about one main idea.
- The first line of a paragraph is **indented**. There is a space before the first word.

   EXAMPLE:

   Fluffy is my cat. She is four years old. She is black and white. She likes to play with yarn. She likes napping in the sun.

- **Read the paragraphs. Answer the questions.**

   Melinda is studying for her math test. The test is on Friday. Melinda wants to get a good grade on the test. She knows that studying will help her do well on the test.

1. Who is the paragraph about? _____

2. Write the first sentence of the paragraph.

_____

   Today is my wife's birthday. She is 35 years old. She is having a party. Nine people are coming to the party. We will eat cake and visit with each other.

1. What is this paragraph about? _____

_____

2. Write the first sentence of the paragraph.

_____

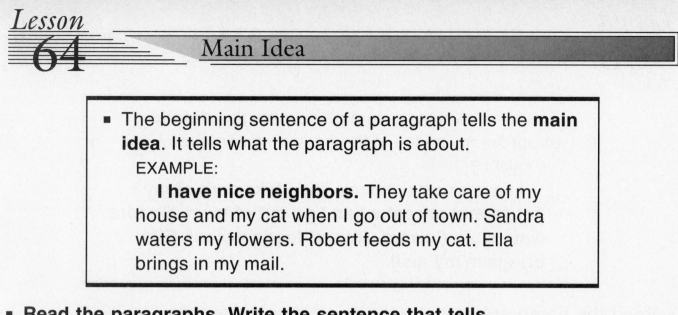

- The beginning sentence of a paragraph tells the **main idea**. It tells what the paragraph is about.
  EXAMPLE:

    I have nice neighbors. They take care of my house and my cat when I go out of town. Sandra waters my flowers. Robert feeds my cat. Ella brings in my mail.

- **Read the paragraphs. Write the sentence that tells the main idea.**

Firefighters are brave people. They go into burning buildings. They put out fires. They teach families how to be safe in their homes.

1. _____

   _____

Lenora found that using a computer can be easy. When Lenora started her new job, she had never used a computer before. She was afraid that it would be hard to use. But Lenora went to a training class. Soon she knew all about computers.

2. _____

   _____

Joe Sanders is a funny man. He tells jokes about elephants. He does magic tricks that don't work. He makes funny faces when he tells stories. He always makes the children laugh.

3. _____

   _____

> - The other sentences in a paragraph give **details** about the main idea in the beginning sentence.
>   EXAMPLE:
>   I have nice neighbors. **They take care of my house and my cat when I go out of town. Sandra waters my flowers. Robert feeds my cat. Ella brings in my mail.**

- **Read the paragraphs. Circle the beginning sentences. Underline the sentences that give details about the main idea.**

Firefighters are brave people. They go into burning buildings. They put out fires. They teach families how to be safe in their homes.

Lenora found that using a computer can be easy. When Lenora started her new job, she had never used a computer before. She was afraid that it would be hard to use. But Lenora went to a training class. Soon she knew all about computers.

Joe Sanders is a funny man. He tells jokes about elephants. He does magic tricks that don't work. He makes funny faces when he tells stories. He always makes the children laugh.

> - The sentences in a paragraph tell things in the order in which they happened.
> - Words like <u>first</u>, <u>second</u>, <u>third</u>, <u>next</u>, <u>then</u>, and <u>last</u> can help tell when things happened.
>   EXAMPLE:
>   Jane got ready for bed. **First**, she took a bath. **Next**, she brushed her teeth. **Then** she put on her pajamas. **Last**, she set her alarm and got into bed.

- **Write 1, 2, 3, or 4 to show what happened first, second, third, and last.**

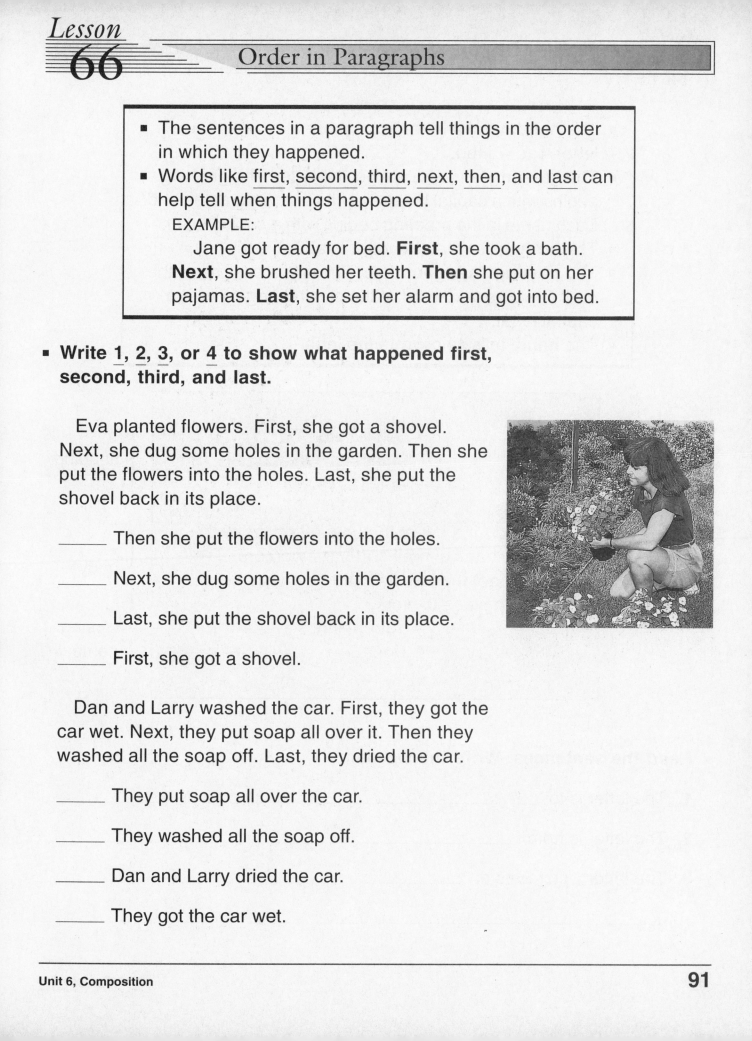

Eva planted flowers. First, she got a shovel. Next, she dug some holes in the garden. Then she put the flowers into the holes. Last, she put the shovel back in its place.

_____ Then she put the flowers into the holes.

_____ Next, she dug some holes in the garden.

_____ Last, she put the shovel back in its place.

_____ First, she got a shovel.

Dan and Larry washed the car. First, they got the car wet. Next, they put soap all over it. Then they washed all the soap off. Last, they dried the car.

_____ They put soap all over the car.

_____ They washed all the soap off.

_____ Dan and Larry dried the car.

_____ They got the car wet.

- The **heading** of a letter tells where and when the letter was written.
- The **greeting** tells who will get the letter. The greeting begins with a capital letter and has a comma at the end. Each name in the greeting begins with a capital letter.
- The **body** tells what the letter is about.
- The **closing** says good-bye. There is a comma at the end. Only the first word of the closing begins with a capital letter.
- The **name** tells who wrote the letter.

608 Weston Dr.
Markham, Ontario L3R 1E5   } heading
Apr. 12, 19___

greeting ——→ Dear Chris,

    I applied for a job at the post office today. I saw large bags of mail and busy workers.
    I hope I get the job. It would be a very interesting place to work.   } body

        Your friend, ←——————— closing
        Rose ←——————————— name

- **Read the sentences. Write the words.**

1. The letter is to _____.

2. The letter is from _____.

3. The letter writer lives at _____

_____.

Planning a Letter

> - Before you write a letter, think about **who** you will write to.
> - Before you write a letter, think **what** you want to write about.

- **Who would you like to write to? Circle the names of the people. Write the names of other people you could send a letter to.**

  1. your husband
  2. your wife
  3. your cousin
  4. your niece

  5. your nephew
  6. a friend
  7. a nice neighbor
  8. your doctor

  9. _____
  10. _____
  11. _____
  12. _____

- **What would you write about in your letter? Circle the ideas you might write about. Then list other ideas you might write about.**

  1. something you did with a friend
  2. a party you went to
  3. a new friend you met
  4. something you did at work
  5. a sport you enjoy

  6. _____
  7. _____
  8. _____
  9. _____
  10. _____

- **Complete the sentences.**

  1. I would write a letter to _____.

  2. I would write about _____

  _____.

- A **friendly letter** tells news.
- A friendly letter has a heading, greeting, body, closing, and name.
- Indent the first line of the body.

711 Short St.
Bluff, UT 84512
Oct. 17, 19___

Dear Pat,
   I just found out some good news. We are moving in June! I will still work at the same place. We are only moving across town.
                    Your friend,
                    Anna Gomez

- **Copy the friendly letter.**

_____

_____

_____

_____

_____

_____

_____

_____

- An envelope has two **addresses**.
- One address tells where the letter is going. It is in the middle of the envelope.
- The **return address** tells who wrote the letter and where the writer lives. It is in the top left corner of the envelope.

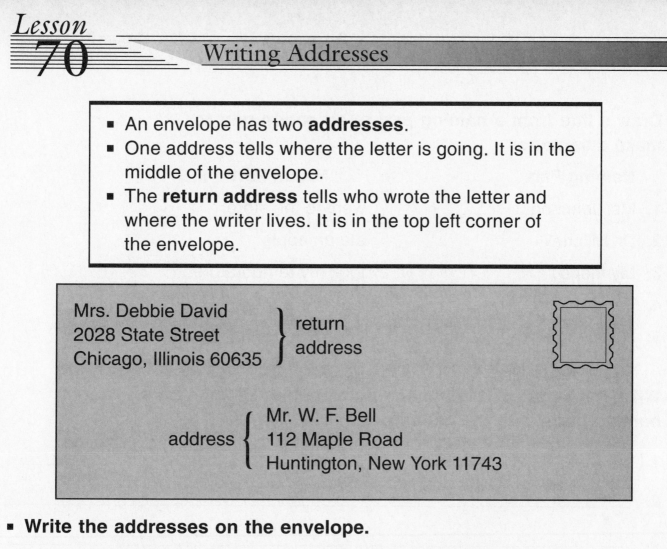

Mrs. Debbie David
2028 State Street
Chicago, Illinois 60635 } return address

address { Mr. W. F. Bell
112 Maple Road
Huntington, New York 11743

- **Write the addresses on the envelope.**

1. **From:** Miss Anna Gomez
711 Short Street
Bluff, Utah 84512

2. **To:** Ms. Pat Murray
704 Heard Road
Akron, Ohio 44309

- **Draw a line from a naming part to an action part to make a sentence.**

Naming Part	Action Part
1. Ms. Johnson	went to the store.
2. Dr. Mitchell	ate an apple.
3. My friend	took my temperature.
4. Pam's niece	looked for the book.
5. Jesse Garza	called last night

- **Write the sentences you made by matching the naming parts with the action parts.**

1. _____

2. _____

3. _____

4. _____

5. _____

- **Read the paragraph. Answer the questions.**

    Lauren and Yuko wanted to go to a movie.
They could not decide what they wanted to
see. They looked at the newspaper. Finally,
they chose a movie.

1. What is this paragraph about? _____

2. Write the first sentence of the paragraph. _____

_____

- **Read the paragraph. Circle the sentence that gives the main idea. Underline the sentences that give details about the main idea.**

I need to clean my apartment this weekend. I will dust. Then I will vacuum the carpet. Next, I will polish all of the wooden furniture. Finally, I will wash the windows.

- **Write heading, greeting, body, closing, and name where they belong. Then circle the letters that should be capital letters. Put commas where they are needed.**

608 Weston Dr.

Markham, Ontario L3R 1E5

Apr. 12, 19___

_____ → dear chris

I got the job I wrote to you about. I will start next Monday. I am really excited about this job. I think I will really like it. I'll let you know how my first day goes.

your friend ← _____

rose ← _____

- Write a friendly letter to someone you know.

- Write your return address in the heading.

- Write today's date in the heading.

- Write <u>Dear</u> _____ in the greeting.

- In the body, talk about work, your friends, things you like to do, or places you like to visit.

- Write a closing that you like.

- Write your name below the closing.

- Check your spelling. Check to see that you used commas and capital letters where needed.

- **Now think about the envelope for your friendly letter.**

  1. Where are you sending the letter?

  _____

  _____

  _____

  2. What is your return address?

  _____

  _____

  _____

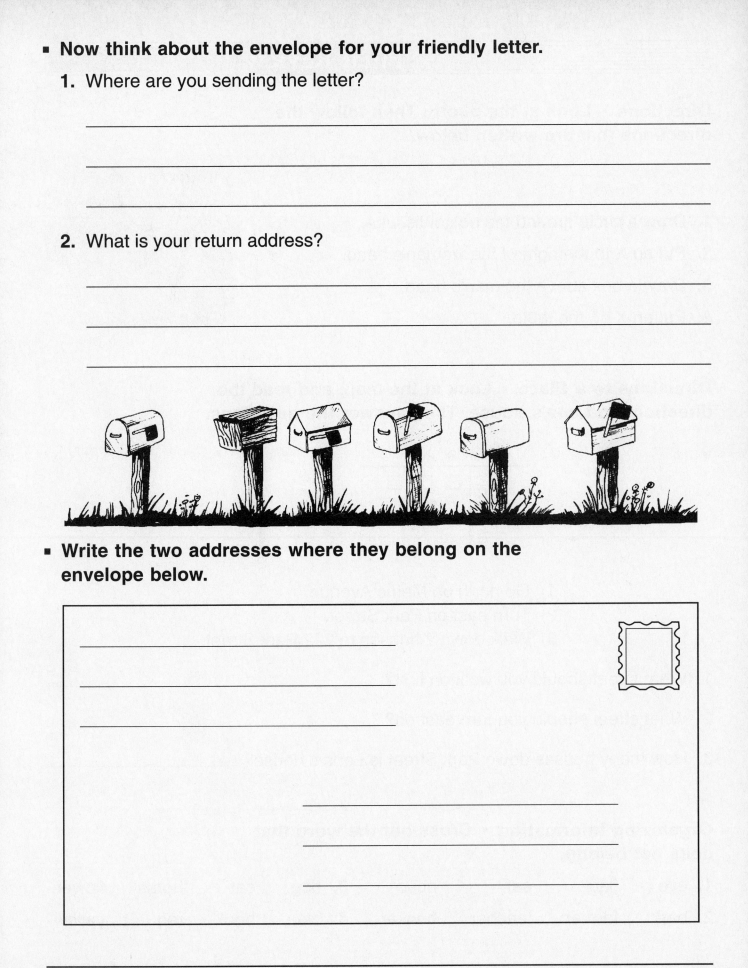

- **Write the two addresses where they belong on the envelope below.**

Directions • **Look at the photo. Then follow the directions that are written below.**

1. Draw a circle around the box of tissues.

2. Put an X to the right of the woman's head.

3. Draw a box above the man's head.

4. Put an X on the table.

Directions to a Place • **Look at the map, and read the directions to Lena's house. Then answer the questions.**

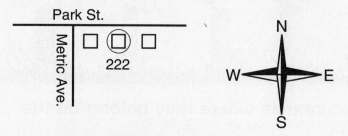

Park St.

Metric Ave.

222

N

W   E

S

1) Go north on Metric Avenue.
2) Turn east on Park Street.
3) Walk down 2 houses to 222 Park Street.

1. What street should you walk on first? _____

2. What street should you turn east on? _____

3. How many houses down Park Street is Lena's house? _____

Organizing Information • **Cross out the word that does not belong.**

1. eye   flag   ear   nose   3. dog   cat   horse   flower

2. bark   farmer   teacher   banker   4. blue   book   red   yellow

Alphabetical Order ▪ **Number the words in alphabetical order. Then write the words in alphabetical order.**

1. _____ chair   _____   2. _____ nest   _____

   _____ hot   _____   _____ penny   _____

   _____ angry   _____   _____ off   _____

Guide Words ▪ **Underline the words that would be on the same page as the guide words.**

                    old / sea

1. toast   poor   village   quack

2. nest   really   tonight   pair

Using a Dictionary ▪ **Use the dictionary words to answer the questions.**

baby a very young child	**broken** 1. not working
birthday the day someone was born	2. in many pieces

1. What word has two meanings? _____

2. What word means "a very young child"? _____

3. What does birthday mean? _____

Table of Contents ▪ **Answer the questions about the table of contents shown below.**

Table of Contents

Why Forts and Castles Were Built..5   Types of Castles...................23

Types of Forts 12   Famous Forts and Castles ..34

1. What is this book about? _____

2. On what pages can you read about types of forts? _____

3. On what page can you read about famous forts and castles? _____

Vocabulary ▪ **Draw a line under the correct word to complete each sentence.**

1. A word that rhymes with <u>cold</u> is (hold, pass).

2. A word that rhymes with <u>coat</u> is (hat, boat).

3. A word that rhymes with <u>bat</u> is (ball, pat).

4. The opposite of <u>clean</u> is (dirty, old).

5. The opposite of <u>quick</u> is (slow, fast).

6. The opposite of <u>easy</u> is (simple, hard).

7. <u>Happy</u> means almost the same as (sad, glad).

8. <u>Sick</u> means almost the same as (well, ill).

9. <u>Yell</u> means almost the same as (smile, shout).

10. Did you (hear, here) the good news about Jeff?

11. He is coming (hear, here) to visit us.

12. I can hardly wait until he is (hear, here).

13. The workers will do (their, there) best.

14. (Their, There) will be lots of people here.

15. You can put the tools (their, there).

16. Did you know the (right, write) answers?

17. I will (right, write) you a letter.

18. You should turn (right, write) at the next intersection.

19. Shelly paid (to, too, two) dollars to park in the parking lot.

20. I had (to, too, two) go to the store.

21. I'd like (to, too, two) make a special dinner.

22. Is it (to, too, two) late to go to the bank?

23. Dennis will be back in (to, too, two) minutes.

Words With Two Meanings · **Look at each pair of photos. Read each sentence. Then write the letter of the correct meaning on the line.**

cook

a.   b.

1. _____ The restaurant is looking for a new cook.

2. _____ Maria will cook dinner in one hour.

3. _____ Juan wants to be a cook in a French restaurant.

4. _____ Your brother is a wonderful cook!

fly

a.   b.

5. _____ My friend will fly to Canada.

6. _____ Would you like to fly in an airplane?

7. _____ The fly keeps buzzing by my ear.

8. _____ The frog ate the fly.

bank

a.   b.

9. _____ Frank got some cash from the bank.

10. _____ My friend and I had a picnic lunch on the bank.

11. _____ What time does the bank close?

12. _____ The bridge connects the east bank to the west bank.

Sentences ▪ Write <u>yes</u> if the group of words is a sentence. Write <u>no</u> if the group of words is not a sentence.

_____ **1.** Look at the plants.　　_____ **4.** Came from the sky.

_____ **2.** Six tiny beans.　　_____ **5.** The plants will grow.

_____ **3.** It is raining.　　_____ **6.** The sunshine will.

Sentence Order ▪ Write these words in an order that makes sense.

1. was table Milk the on

_____

2. from Butter comes milk

_____

3. Cheese milk also comes from

_____

4. Joanna to drink likes milk

_____

5. spilled his milk Her son

_____

Telling or Asking Sentences ▪ Write <u>T</u> for telling sentences. Write <u>A</u> for asking sentences.

1. _____ Is Hoan home from work?　　**5.** _____ She went to the library.

2. _____ He has to work late.　　**6.** _____ Why did she go to the library?

3. _____ He works hard.　　**7.** _____ She wants to check out a book.

4. _____ Where did Jackie go?　　**8.** _____ Jackie will be right back.

Naming Part · Choose the naming part to complete each sentence.

| Phillip | The dirty dishes | My family | The house | Katie and Kathy |

1. _____ works together to clean the house.

2. _____ dusts the bookshelves in his room.

3. _____ do the laundry.

4. _____ need to be washed.

5. _____ looks very clean now.

Action Part · Choose the action part to complete each sentence.

| sounds angry | looks better over the table | tastes sweet |
| feels rough | smells sour | |

1. The orange _____ .

2. A lemon _____ .

3. The sandpaper _____ .

4. That man _____ .

5. The painting _____ .

Sentence Parts · Circle the naming part of each sentence. Draw a line under the action part of each sentence.

1. Jerald and Brad surprised Paula.

2. The young men flew into town for the week.

3. Brad knocked on Paula's door.

4. Paula hugged her two friends.

5. Some of Paula's neighbors met her two friends.

Nouns or Verbs ▪ Write noun or verb for each underlined word.

1. My birthday was today. _____

2. I opened my presents. _____

3. There was a new shirt in one box. _____

4. My husband will buy me a new dishwasher. _____

Proper Nouns ▪ Write each proper noun on the line.

1. Ms. Grayson is our new neighbor. _____

2. We just moved to Atlanta. _____

3. I have never lived in Georgia before. _____

Plural Nouns ▪ Rewrite these nouns to make them mean more than one.

1. tree _____   4. bush _____

2. car _____   5. lunch _____

3. glass _____   6. fox _____

Verbs ▪ Write the correct verb on the line.

1. Koji _____ the dog before breakfast.   (walked, walking)

2. He is _____ on his tax return.   (worked, working)

3. Koji _____ his wife to help him with the tax return.   (asked, asking)

4. Akiko is _____ for work.   (dressed, dressing)

5. Akiko _____ Koji when she got home from work.   (helped, helping)

Using the Correct Word ▪ Draw a line under the correct word.

1. Last Monday, Janet and Tony (run, ran) on the track.

2. Stephanie (was, were) at the city park.

3. Brenda (see, saw) the actors perform.

4. Matt (has, have, had) a cut on his hand last Monday.

5. Joe and (I, me) were at the library.

6. (Is, Are) you going to the movie?

7. That movie (played, playing) last November.

8. Dr. Guzman (give, gave) me tickets.

9. We are going to (an, a) early show.

10. (Do, Does) you want to go with me?

Pronouns ▪ Rewrite the sentences. Use a pronoun in place of the underlined words. You will use some pronouns more than once.

He	She	It	We	They

1. José and Laura planned a party.

   _____

2. The party was for Steve's birthday.

   _____

3. Laura invited the guests.

   _____

4. Kamal and I helped put up decorations.

   _____

5. José made the cake.

   _____

6. Steve was very surprised.

   _____

Capitalization ▪ Circle the letters that should be capital letters.

1. mr. w. c. sanchez works at harris school.

2. mr. kelly took his class to riverside park.

3. they will go to the hudson river in september.

4. will grandfather come to see aunt ruth?

5. did uncle bill come for thanksgiving?

6. donna took a boat ride on lake erie last summer.

7. donna and i met ms. h. m. slade last fall.

8. we went to a party for mrs. lee in november.

Abbreviations and Contractions ▪ Draw a line from each word to its short form.

1. March	Sat.	5. January	Wed.
2. is not	Mar.	6. Sunday	don't
3. December	isn't	7. do not	Sun.
4. Saturday	Dec.	8. Wednesday	Jan.

Place Names ▪ Rewrite the place names. Use abbreviations.

1. hanson drive _____

2. baker road _____

3. second street _____

Book Titles ▪ Write these book titles correctly.

1. forts and castles _____

2. the firm _____

Punctuation ▪ **Write the sentences correctly. Put periods, question marks, and commas where needed.**

1. What will you do in Reno Nevada

   _____

2. Who is with Dr Trigo

   _____

3. It is Mr V F Casey

   _____

4. He was born on March 20 1974

   _____

5. He likes to read dance and sing

   _____

6. His family moved there on June 4 1978

   _____

7. I will be out of town in March April and May

   _____

8. Did Ms Kirkpatrick go to San Francisco California

   _____

9. The parade will be on New Year's Day

   _____

10. Dr Nguyen will be in town on Nov 12

    _____

11. How can we get to Santa Fe New Mexico

    _____

12. Miss Hall will be late on Monday Wednesday and Friday

    _____

Naming and Action Parts ▪ Draw a line from a
naming part to an action part to make a sentence.

Naming Part	Action Part
1. Miss Abrams	went to the park.
2. Frank's brother	has a vegetable garden.
3. Mr. Yancy	works for my husband.

Sentences ▪ Write the sentences you made by
matching the naming parts with the action parts.

1. _____

2. _____

3. _____

Paragraphs ▪ Read the paragraphs. Circle the
sentence that gives the main idea. Underline the
sentences that give details about the main idea.

   1.   Baseball is a sport I like very much. I like to play

        on the city team in the summer. I've been saving

        baseball cards since I was five. I like to watch

        games at night. I have a great time at the ballpark.

   2.   Richard wanted to look good for his job interview.

        The day before the interview he bought some new

        clothes. He hung his new clothes in the closet so

        they would not get wrinkled.

Order in Paragraphs ▪ Write 1, 2, 3, or 4 to show what happened first, second, third, and last.

> Amy made her bed. First, she pulled up the top sheet. Next, she made the blanket even on all sides. Then she shook the pillow. Last, she laid the quilt across the bed.

_____ Then she shook the pillow.

_____ Next, she made the blanket even on all sides.

_____ Last, she laid the quilt across the bed.

_____ First, she pulled up the top sheet.

Addresses ▪ Write the two addresses where they belong on the envelope below.

1. From: Mr. J. T. Conners
4203 Greystone Drive
Cincinnati, OH 45236

2. To: Marla Franklin
1121 Sunset Road
Colorado Springs, CO 80919

A. Look at the photo. Follow the directions.

1. Put an X on the helmet.

2. Put an X to the left of the helmet.

3. Put an X below the helmet.

4. Draw a circle around the helmet.

B. Look at the map, and read the directions to Anna's house. Then answer the questions.

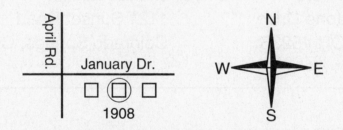

1) Go south on April Road.
2) Turn east on January Drive.
3) Walk down two houses to 1908 January Drive.

1. What direction should you go first? _____

2. What street should you walk on first? _____

3. Which direction should you turn? _____

4. What street should you turn on? _____

5. How many houses down January Drive is Anna's house? _____

C. Cross out the word that does not belong.

1. snow   mud   sleet   rain

2. April   July   Tuesday   November

3. couch   truck   desk   bed

D. Write the words in alphabetical order.

1. Carlos _____

    Patty _____

    Nadia _____

2. lake _____

    river _____

    ocean _____

E. Circle the words that would be on the same page as the guide words.

joke / lost

1. park   key   shop   quit

2. today   could   lamp   move

3. jump   ice   meat   cost

F. Use the dictionary words to answer the questions.

> **can** a container made out of metal
>
> **change** to make different
>
> **chop** 1. to cut with an ax
> 2. a piece of meat

1. What word has two meanings? _____

2. What word means "to make different"? _____

3. What is a can made out of? _____

G. Read the words in the box. Then follow the directions.

near	tiny	asleep	rake	smooth	run

1. Write the words from the box that rhyme.

   lake _____   ton _____

2. Write the words from the box that mean almost the same.

   flat _____   small _____

3. Write the words from the box that mean the opposite.

   far _____   awake _____

H. Circle the correct word to complete each sentence.

1. Gina and Robert ate (to, too, two) much.

2. I (hear, here) they both have upset stomachs.

3. It will take a while for (there, their) stomachs to feel better.

I. Write T before the telling sentence. Write A before the asking sentence. Write X before the group of words that is not a sentence. Circle the naming parts. Underline the action parts.

_____ 1. Will you swim today?

_____ 2. Molly swims at the city pool.

_____ 3. On weekends.

J. Circle the special naming words. Underline the action words.

1. Ms. Allison works in a factory.

2. She goes every Sunday and Monday.

K. Circle the word that best completes each sentence.

1. Anne (was, were) taking the bus to work.

2. (She, It) got on the bus that was headed downtown.

3. Anne took (a, an) elevator up to her office.

4. The other workers (is, are) arriving, too.

L. Circle each letter that should be a capital. Write the correct punctuation marks for each sentence.

1. can you go with ms mary a barnes to a store on first street

2. she wants to go to a big sale at the store this friday saturday and sunday

3. we didnt find any good bargains there last april

M. Read the paragraph. Circle the main idea and underline the details.

José needed to get to work right away. He got into his car.

Then he started the engine and drove to his office. He got

to work right on time.

_____

Below is a list of the sections on *Check What You've Learned* and the pages on which the skills in each section are taught. If you missed any questions, turn to the pages listed and practice the skills. Then correct the problems you missed on *Check What You've Learned*.

Section	Practice Page	Section	Practice Page	Section	Practice Page
Unit 1		*Unit 2*		*Unit 5*	
A	5–8	G	23–25	L	68–73, 77–79, 82
B	9	H	26–28	*Unit 6*	
C	11	*Unit 3*		M	88–90
D	13	I	34, 36–42		
E	14	*Unit 4*			
F	15–17	J	47–48, 50–51		
		K	53–54, 60, 62		

Check What You Know (P. 1)

A. The following should be done:
1. put an X on the apple
2. put an X to the right of the apple
3. put an X above the apple
4. draw a circle around the apple

B.
1. east   4. Dolphin Drive
2. Shark Road   5. two
3. south

Check What You Know (P. 2)

C. 1. pen   2. name   3. door

D.
1. Carol
   Thomas
   Zena
2. carpet
   door
   window

E. 1. dear   2. egg   3. dust

F.
1. bill
2. box
3. to heat a liquid until bubbles form

Check What You Know (P. 3)

G. 1. knew, pan   3. short, narrow
     2. angry, big

H. 1. to   2. hear   3. there

I. The words in bold should be circled.
1. A, am, I   3. T, I, bought
2. X

J. The words in bold should be circled.
1. **Mr. Donaldson**, grows
2. plants, **April**

Check What You Know (P. 4)

K. 1. were   2. We   3. a   4. are

L. The letters in bold should be circled, and punctuation marks should be added as shown.
1. **m**r. **t**. **r**. **w**iggins and **i** went to **d**aytona **b**each last **s**aturday, **s**unday, and **m**onday.
2. **r**honda went to the beach last **a**ugust.
3. **d**idn't she take her cat named **w**hiskers?

M. The sentence in bold should be circled.
     Julia wanted to bake her friend a cake for his birthday. First, Julia read the recipe. Then she baked the cake. After the cake cooled, she put frosting on it.

Unit 1   Study Skills

Lesson 1, Listening for Directions (P. 5)

The following should be done:
1. put an H to the left of the woman's head
2. put an A above the woman's head
3. draw a circle around the letter
4. draw a circle around the photo on the table
5. put an X on the envelope

Lesson 2, More Listening for Directions (P. 6)

The following key words should be written:
1. 1) pick up dry cleaning
     2) vacuum living room
     3) feed cat

2. 1) south on Red Road
   2) west on Green Street
   3) two houses to 4202 Green Street

Lesson 3, Following Directions (P. 7)

There should be an X in the following places, and the words in the dark boxes should be written:

1. above the tire; above
2. on the tire; on
3. under the tire; under
4. inside the tire; inside
5. beside the tire, on the left; beside; left
6. beside the tire, on the right; beside; right

Lesson 4, Following Written Directions (P. 8)

The following should be done:
1. circle the button on the left
2. circle the safe on the right
3. draw a box around the teeth, the feet, and the elbow
4. circle the umbrella that does not have a handle
5. circle the letters shown in bold
   D **B** G D **B** P R **B**
6. put an X on the letters in bold
   n r **m** **m** w **m** n v

Lesson 5, Following Directions to a Place (P. 9)

1. south
2. Fifth Avenue
3. east
4. Main Street
5. 5

Lesson 6, Making Comparisons (P. 10)

1. Jackie
2. Andrew
3. Andrew
4. Jackie
5. Andrew
6. Jackie
7. Andrew
8. Jackie
9. Andrew
10. Jackie

Lesson 7, Organizing Information (P. 11)

Top:
The following should be crossed out:
1. turtle
2. dog
3. computer
4. sink
5. woman
6. popcorn
7. candle
8. mud
9. sock
10. blue

Bottom:

Foods	Names	Actions
apple	Andy	eat
bread	Jenny	type
rice	Vince	write
potato	Lupe	sing
cheese	Dennis	talk
grapes	Rudy	dance

Lesson 8, Letters in Alphabetical Order (P. 12)

Discuss your answers with your instructor.

1. U	4. R	7. X	10. Q
2. J	5. O	8. G	11. F
3. D	6. M	9. Z	12. L

1. K	4. G	7. U	10. B
2. F	5. X	8. N	11. M
3. R	6. D	9. T	12. E

1. A	4. W	7. K	10. R
2. S	5. I	8. G	11. U
3. M	6. E	9. P	12. J

Lesson 9, Words in Alphabetical Order (P. 13)

1. 2, 1, 3   air, bag, car
2. 3, 2, 1   rock, sea, tool
3. 2, 3, 1   dog, egg, fish
4. 2, 3, 1   gate, hat, ice
5. 1, 3, 2   joke, king, lake
6. 2, 3, 1   mail, neck, owl
7. 3, 1, 2   us, very, well
8. 2, 3, 1   x-ray, yes, zoo
9. 3, 2, 1   nail, oak, pan
10. 1, 3, 2   quit, rug, sun

Lesson 10, Finding Words in a Dictionary (P. 14)

Top:
1. baby   2. bed

Bottom:
1. see / sit   4. fit / fun
2. fit / fun   5. rain / run
3. rain / run   6. see / sit

Lesson 11, Using a Dictionary (P. 15)

1. middle   5. many
2. paw   6. neighbor
3. open   7. to go back
4. noise   8. never used before

Lesson 11, Using a Dictionary (P. 16)

1. no   6. yes
2. yes   7. yes
3. no   8. no
4. yes   9. no
5. no   10. no

Lesson 12, More Than One Meaning (P. 17)

Top:

The words in bold should be circled.
1. **not warm**
2. a sickness of the nose and throat

1. **to fasten together with string**
2. a cloth worn around the neck

1. **moving water**
2. to move the hands back and forth as a greeting

Bottom:
1. tie   1
2. tie   2
3. wave   1
4. wave   2
5. cold   1
6. cold   2

Lesson 13, Table of Contents (P. 18)

1. Plants
2. 21, 22, 23
3. 7, 8
4. 15, 16
5. Grasses
6. Medicines from Plants
7. 32, 33
8. 34
9. Fruits
10. Grains

Review (P. 19)

Top:

The following should be done:
1. put an X on the saw; draw a circle around the hat; put an X above the hat; and draw a box around the saw

Middle:
1. 1) storm in an hour
   2) flash floods
   3) stay tuned; roads closed

Bottom:
1. south
2. April Drive
3. 3

Review (P. 20)

The following words should be crossed out:
1. help
2. read

1. 1, 3, 2   almost, hot, peanut
2. 3, 2, 1   teach, you, zipper
3. 2, 1, 3   and, point, town
4. 1, 3, 2   track, voice, wear

1. job
2. hard

1. poor
2. orange

Using What You've Learned (P. 21)

Top:

The following should be done:
1. write Mr. on the man
2. write Mrs. on the woman
3. put an X on the pot that has food cooking in it
4. draw a circle around the spice rack
5. put an X to the left of the basket that is hanging on the wall
6. write stove on the stove

Bottom:

Foods	Kitchen Items
carrots	knife
meat	spoon
potatoes	pot

Using What You've Learned (P. 22)

Top:
1. 2
2. 1

Middle:
1. Writing
2. 13, 14
3. 32
4. Fiction Books
5. Newspaper Articles

Bottom:
1. airplane
   bake
   dish
   face
2. gold
   lake
   moon
   pond

Unit 2 Vocabulary

Lesson 14, Words That Rhyme (P. 23)

Top:
1. mop
2. ring
3. door
4. dish
5. ship
6. luck

Bottom:
1. pail
2. bake
3. tar
4. cash
5. way
6. pest
7. cone
8. mess

Lesson 15, Words That Mean the Same (P. 24)

1. road
2. home
3. twisted
4. sad
5. sick
6. recall
7. sound
8. lamp
9. middle
10. yelled
11. supper
12. great

Lesson 16, Words That Mean the Opposite (P. 25)

Top:
1. soft
2. long
3. dark
4. on
5. happy
6. low

Bottom:
1. dry
2. slow
3. bad
4. cold
5. go
6. hard
7. dirty
8. no

Lesson 17, Words That Sound the Same (P. 26)

Top:
1. hear
2. here
3. here
4. hear
5. here
6. here

Bottom:
1. their
2. their
3. there
4. their
5. their

Lesson 18, More Words That Sound the Same (P. 27)

Top:
1. write
2. right
3. right
4. write
5. right
6. write
7. write
8. right
9. right
10. write
11. right

Bottom:

Discuss your answers with your instructor.

Lesson 19, Other Words That Sound the Same (P. 28)

1. to
2. two
3. to
4. to
5. to
6. too
7. too
8. two
9. to
10. two
11. to
12. to
13. too
14. to

Lesson 20, Words That Have Two Meanings (P. 29)

1. a
2. b
3. a
4. b
5. b
6. a
7. a
8. b
9. b
10. a
11. b
12. b

Review (P. 30)

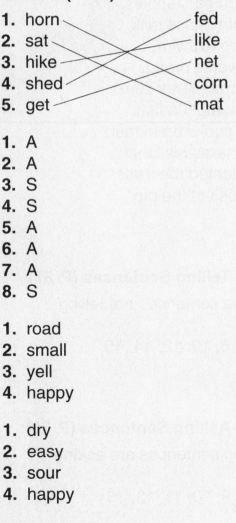

1. horn — corn
2. sat — net
3. hike — fed
4. shed — mat
5. get — like

1. A
2. A
3. S
4. S
5. A
6. A
7. A
8. S

1. road
2. small
3. yell
4. happy

1. dry
2. easy
3. sour
4. happy

Review (P. 31)

Top:

1. their
2. hear
3. here
4. hear
5. there
6. too
7. to
8. write
9. two

Bottom:

1. a
2. b
3. b
4. a

Using What You've Learned (P. 32)

Top:

1. Walk up the stairs.
2. Take two big (or large) steps.
3. Open the door.
4. Turn on the light.
5. Find the new shirt.
6. Find a small (or little) box in the pocket.

Bottom:

Discuss your answers with your instructor.

Using What You've Learned (P. 33)

> July 5, 1994
>
> Dear Rosa and Marcos,
>
>   Hear I am in Florida. I wanted too right you a letter two tell you about my trip.
>
>   Their are many interesting things too do and see while I am hear. The thing I like best is going two here different bands play each night.
>
>   I'll see you in too weeks.
>
>   Sincerely,
>   Randy

July 5, 1994

Dear Rosa and Marcos,

Here I am in Florida. I wanted to write you a letter to tell you about my trip.

There are many interesting things to do and see while I am here. The thing I like best is going to hear different bands play each night.

I'll see you in two weeks.

Sincerely,
Randy

Unit 3 Sentences

Lesson 21, Sentences (P. 34)

1. no
2. yes
3. no
4. yes
5. yes
6. yes
7. no
8. no
9. yes
10. yes
11. yes
12. no
13. yes
14. no
15. no
16. yes

Lesson 22, More Sentences (P. 35)

Top:

1. Mrs. Brown lives on my street.
2. Our building is made of wood.
3. Four families live in our building.
4. Our company had a picnic.
5. The food tasted great.

6. The sun shone all day.
7. Corn and beans grow on a farm.
8. The wagon has a broken wheel.
9. The mother goat fed the baby goat.
10. The boat sailed in strong winds.
11. The fisher caught seven fish.
12. Some of the fish were sold in the store.
13. Our team won ten games.
14. Our batters hit the ball a lot.
15. The ballpark was full of fans.

Bottom:

Discuss your answers with your instructor.

Lesson 23, Word Order in Sentences (P. 36)

1. My friend eats apples.
2. Elizabeth drinks milk.
3. Kim likes to swim.
4. Justin wants bread.
5. Ms. Carter plants corn.
6. Chang caught a fish.
7. Shawn cooks breakfast.
8. Hoan shares his lunch.
9. Rosa planted the tree.
10. Kate looks at the pie.

Lesson 24, Telling Sentences (P. 37)

The following sentences are telling sentences:

1, 2, 4, 5, 7, 8, 10, 12, 14, 15

Lesson 25, Asking Sentences (P. 38)

The following sentences are asking sentences:

1, 2, 4, 6, 7, 9, 10, 11, 13, 15

Lesson 26, Kinds of Sentences (P. 39)

Top:

1. telling
2. asking
3. telling
4. asking
5. telling
6. telling
7. asking
8. telling
9. asking
10. telling

Bottom:

Telling Sentences

I went to the store.
I bought some carrots.

Asking Sentences

What did you buy?
Are there any vegetables?

Lesson 27, Naming Part of Sentences (P. 40)

The following parts of each sentence should be circled:

1. My family and I
2. Sally Harper
3. Miss Jenkins
4. Mr. and Mrs. Avalos
5. Henry
6. Mr. Byrne
7. Mrs. Lee
8. Dr. Diaz
9. Jeanine
10. Mr. Wolf
11. Sam Taft
12. Ms. O'Dowd
13. Nina
14. Some families
15. Mrs. Clark
16. Carolyn and Albert
17. Julie

Lesson 28, Action Part of Sentences (P. 41)

The following parts of each sentence should be circled:

1. live on a busy street
2. goes to vote
3. drives very slowly
4. walk their dog
5. swings his racket
6. cuts his grass
7. picks up her children
8. shops for food
9. walks in the park
10. brings the mail
11. reads the newspaper
12. cooks dinner
13. paints the house
14. plant a garden
15. washes her windows
16. plant flower seeds
17. waters the garden

Lesson 29, Sentence Parts (P. 42)

Top:

1. Books
2. Music
3. A hammer
4. A pen
5. The watch
6. My telephone
7. Dinner

Bottom:

1. bakes
2. rings
3. overflows
4. stalls
5. ticks
6. reflects
7. shines

Discuss your answers with your instructor.

Review (P. 43)

Top:
1. N
2. S
3. S
4. N

Middle:
1. Alan and Ellen — teaches them how to play.
2. The big game — is Saturday night.
3. Their coach — play on the same team.

4. The phone — is calling from Toronto.
5. Our friend — rush to answer it.
6. Betty and Tom — rings.

7. The hungry frog — ate an insect.
8. Twenty geese — curled up to sleep.
9. A cat — flew south for the winter.

Bottom:
1. Tom is a good friend.
2. He lives next door.
3. We drive to work together.

Review (P. 44)

Top:
1. asking
2. asking
3. telling
6. telling
7. telling
8. asking
10. telling
12. asking

Bottom:
1. Many people go out to eat after work.
2. Amanda and Jeff go to a restaurant.
3. Amanda orders her favorite meal.
4. Jeff tries something new.

Using What You've Learned (P. 45)

The following sentences should be circled and written:
1. Would you like to work on an airplane?
2. Have you ever flown on an airplane?
3. How was the food on the airplane?
4. Did your cousin enjoy the flight?
5. How do you get a job with an airline?
6. May I go with you?

Using What You've Learned (P. 46)

Top:
1. A big airport is a busy place.
2. Many airplanes are very big.
3. The people on airplanes wear seat belts.
4. A pilot flies the airplane.
5. Many airport workers work very hard.

Bottom:
1. The pilot is my friend.
2. She flies around the world.
3. She sees many countries.
4. I sat in the pilot's seat.
5. The airport is very big.
6. It is easy to get lost.
7. I would like to fly.

Lesson 30, Naming Words (P. 47)

Top:

1. apple
2. bird
3. box
4. car
5. chair
6. desk
7. grass
8. pen
9. rug
10. tree
11. truck
12. woman

Bottom:

1. The cook boiled an egg.   cook, egg
2. A bird flies to the tree.   bird, tree
3. A chair is by the desk.   chair, desk
4. A man sits in the chair.   man, chair
5. The woman drives a truck.   woman, truck
6. The truck is on the highway.   truck, highway

Lesson 31, Special Naming Words (P. 48)

Top:

1. Bob's Bakery
2. Bridge Road
3. China
4. Elf Corn
5. Gabriel
6. Ms. Valdez
7. New York City
8. Ohio
9. Pat Green
10. State Street

Bottom:

1. I bought apples at Hill's Store.   Hill's Store
2. The store is on Baker Street.   Baker Street
3. It is near Stone Library.   Stone Library
4. I gave an umbrella to Emily Fuller.   Emily Fuller

Lesson 32, One and More Than One (P. 49)

Top:

1. hats
2. chairs
3. belts
4. trees
5. flags
6. jets

Middle:

1. lunches
2. dresses
3. glasses
4. dishes
5. boxes
6. watches

Bottom:

1. ponds
2. pigs
3. brushes
4. logs
5. wishes
6. benches
7. axes
8. buttons

Lesson 33, Action Words (P. 50)

Top:
1. The dogs — bark.
2. The baby — cries.
3. The wind — blows.
4. The birds — sing.
5. The man — reads.

Bottom:
1. jogs
2. work
3. say
4. likes
5. waves
6. stops
7. looks
8. waits
9. crosses
10. passes
11. honks
12. hears
13. drives

Lesson 34, Naming Word or Action Word (P. 51)

Top:
1. clerk; store
2. scale; vegetables
3. shelves; food
4. groceries; sack

Middle:
1. takes
2. puts
3. pours
4. rubs
5. vacuums

Bottom:
1. verb
2. noun
3. noun
4. verb
5. noun
6. noun
7. verb
8. noun
9. verb

Lesson 35, Adding *-ed* or *-ing* to Verbs (P. 52)

Top:
1. bowled
2. called
3. wanted
4. inviting
5. jumped
6. scored
7. clapping
8. asking
9. smiling
10. thanked

Bottom:
1. Carmen is finishing her work now.
2. Carmen helped her husband cook yesterday.
3. Manuel is cooking some soup today.

Lesson 36, Using *Is* or *Are* (P. 53)

Top:
1. are
2. is
3. are
4. is
5. is
6. is
7. are
8. is
9. are

Bottom:

Discuss your answers with your instructor.

Bottom:
1. saw   Last week we saw Lee at the movie theater.
2. sees   Now Lee sees us at the store.

Lesson 37, Using *Was* or *Were* (P. 54)

Top:
1. were
2. was
3. were
4. was
5. were
6. were
7. was
8. were
9. was

Bottom:

Discuss your answers with your instructor.

Lesson 38, Using *See*, *Sees*, or *Saw* (P. 55)

Top:
1. sees or saw
2. see
3. sees
4. sees
5. saw
6. saw
7. see
8. saw
9. see
10. see

Lesson 39, Using *Run*, *Runs*, or *Ran* (P. 56)

1. ran   Horses ran wild long ago.
2. run   A horse can run ten miles every day.
3. run   How fast can a horse run?
4. ran   Ms. Brooks ran in a race last week.
5. runs   Mr. Martin runs home from work now.
6. runs   Now Amanda runs with her friend.
7. ran   Yesterday Amanda ran with her husband.

Lesson 40, Using *Give*, *Gives*, or *Gave* (P. 57)

Top:
1. gives
2. gave
3. give
4. gave
5. gave
6. gave
7. gave
8. gave
9. gives
10. give

Bottom:

Discuss your answers with your instructor.

Lesson 41, Using *Do* or *Does* (P. 58)

Top:
1. do
2. does
3. does
4. does
5. does
6. do
7. does
8. do
9. does
10. do
11. do
12. do

Bottom:

Discuss your answers with your instructor.

Lesson 42, Using *Has, Have,* or *Had* (P. 59)

1. had
2. had
3. had
4. had
5. have
6. has
7. have
8. has
9. has
10. have
11. had
12. has
13. had

Lesson 43, Pronouns (P. 60)

1. She got a gift.
2. It was for her birthday.
3. He brought the gift.
4. They went to Alicia's party.
5. We are going to the party.
6. They will bring a surprise.
7. She baked a cake for Alicia.
8. It will end soon.

Lesson 44, Using *I* or *Me* (P. 61)

Top:
1. I
2. me
3. I
4. me
5. I
6. I

Bottom:
1. I
2. I
3. me
4. me
5. I
6. me
7. me
8. I

Lesson 45, Using *A* or *An* (P. 62)

1.	an	13.	an
2.	a	14.	an
3.	a	15.	a
4.	an	16.	a
5.	a	17.	a
6.	an	18.	an
7.	an	19.	an
8.	an	20.	a
9.	a	21.	an
10.	a	22.	an
11.	a	23.	an
12.	a	24.	a

Lesson 46, Using Words That Compare (P. 63)

1. younger   Daryl is younger than Monica.
2. oldest   Kim is the oldest worker in the factory.
3. smaller   A centimeter is smaller than a meter.
4. longest   That trail is the longest one in the park.
5. quieter   Our apartment is quieter than your house.
6. stronger   Mr. Mata is stronger than his son.
7. softest   That blue chair is the softest in the room.

Review (P. 64)

The words in bold should be circled.
1. The **couple** sat on the **beach**.
2. The **sand** hurts their **feet**.
3. **Boats** float on the **waves**.

1. Mr. Harper
2. Colorado
3. Tom Adams Drive
4. Granger Park

1. dresses
2. boxes
3. trees
4. foxes

1. opening
2. pulled
3. playing
4. jumped
5. looking

Review (P. 65)

Top:
1. is
2. were
3. a
4. has
5. runs
6. gave
7. me
8. I
9. an
10. biggest

Middle:
1. see
2. saw
3. do
4. does

Bottom:
1. We went to a movie.
2. They said it was a good movie.
3. She wants to see it again.

Using What You've Learned (P. 66)

John: Jeff and I are twins.

Jeff: We were born on the same day.

John: I am older than Jeff. I was born one minute before Jeff. Our brother James is the oldest of all the children.

Jeff: Our mother was surprised when she saw us. She was not ready for two babies.
Our father was surprised when he saw two of us, too.

John: After we were born, our father ran to the telephone.

Jeff: He called our grandmother.

John: He said, "Do you believe this? Now we have two babies!"

Using What You've Learned (P. 67)

Yesterday <u>was</u> a special day for Robert. He <u>started</u> a new job. His family <u>had</u> a big dinner to celebrate. They were very proud of him.

Everyone in the family helped <u>get</u> dinner ready. Robert said, "Maggie and <u>I</u> will set the table." Tanya and Sharise <u>put</u> the food on the table. The family could <u>see</u> that it was quite a feast.

During dinner, Robert told how <u>he</u> got the job. He said he filled out <u>an</u> application. His application was <u>neater</u> than any of the others. He had <u>an</u> interview. He wore the <u>nicest</u> suit he owned.

Robert <u>liked</u> the woman who interviewed him. The woman could tell Robert would <u>do</u> a great job. She <u>hired</u> him right away.

Unit 5	Capitalization and Punctuation

Lesson 47, Writing Names of People (P. 68)

Top:
1. Mark Twain
2. Bill Clinton
3. Roy Mayers
4. Michael Jordan
5. Leslie Ford

Middle:

The first letter of the following should be circled:
1. mother, grandma
2. grandma, grandpa
3. uncle carlos, aunt kathy

Bottom:
1. Did Dad help Mom?
2. Grandma and I made dinner.
3. Uncle Frank is visiting us.

Lesson 48, Writing Initials (P. 69)

Top:
1. R. L.
2. C. A. C.
3. M. B.
4. M. B.
5. C. F.
6. T. L. T.
7. I. B.
8. L. A. W.

Middle:
1. J. W. A.
2. L. B. Hopkins
3. J. Yolen
4. P. A. R.

Bottom:
1. The box was for M. S. Mills.
2. D. E. Ellis sent it to her.
3. T. J. Lee brought the box to the house.

Lesson 49, Writing Titles of Respect (P. 70)

Top:
1. Mrs. Ruth Scott
2. Mr. Kurt Wiese
3. Miss E. Garcia
4. Dr. Washington
5. Ms. Carol Baylor
6. Mr. and Mrs. H. Cox
7. Miss K. E. Jones

Bottom:
1. Mrs. H. Stone is here to see Dr. Brooks.
2. Dr. Brooks and Ms. Miller are not here.
3. Miss Ari and Mr. Lee came together.
4. Mr. F. Green will go in first.

Lesson 50, Writing Names of Places (P. 71)

Top:
1. James lives on Market Street.
2. I think Thomas Park is in this town.
3. We went to Mathis Lake for a picnic.
4. Is Seton School far away?

Bottom:
1. Webb St.
2. Airport Rd.
3. Doe Dr.
4. Hill Rd.
5. Bell St.
6. Oak Dr.

Lesson 51, Writing Names of Days (P. 72)

Top:
1. Sunday
2. Friday
3. Wednesday
4.-5. Discuss your answers with your instructor.

Bottom:
1. Sunday   Sun.
2. Monday   Mon.
3. Tuesday   Tues.
4. Wednesday   Wed.
5. Thursday   Thurs.
6. Friday   Fri.
7. Saturday   Sat.

Lesson 52, Writing Names of Months (P. 73)

Top:
1. January
2. February
3. March
4. April
5. May
6. June
7. July
8. August
9. September
10. October
11. November
12. December

Bottom:
1. Jan.
2. Mar.
3. Nov.
4. Aug.
5. Sept.
6. Feb.
7. Oct.
8. Dec.
9. Apr.

Lesson 53, Writing Names of Seasons (P. 74)

Top:

winter	spring
December	March
January	April
February	May

summer	fall
June	September
July	October
August	November

Bottom:
1. winter
2. spring
3. summer
4. fall

Lesson 54, Writing Names of Holidays (P. 75)

Top:
1. New Year's Day
2. Mother's Day
3. Independence Day
4. Labor Day
5. Victoria Day
6. Thanksgiving Day

Bottom:
1. January 1 is New Year's Day.
2. I like Valentine's Day.
3. Boxing Day is a British holiday.
4. Father's Day is in June.
5. Thanksgiving is on Thursday.
6. We have a picnic on Independence Day.

Lesson 55, Writing Book Titles (P. 76)

1. The Wonders of Science
2. Protecting Wildlife
3. Conserving the Atmosphere
4. Mathematics in Daily Living
5. Reading for Today
6. Great Disasters
7. Choosing Good Health
8. Waste and Recycling

Lesson 56, Beginning Sentences (P. 77)

1. Deb and Tran work for a book store.
2. Tran answers the phone.
3. He takes the orders called in by customers.
4. Deb types the orders into the computer.
5. She prints out a copy of each order.
6. Then she gives the printouts to Tran.
7. Tran looks at each printout.
8. The printouts show which books have been ordered.
9. Tran packs each order into a box.
10. Then Deb mails the boxes.

Lesson 57, Ending Sentences (P. 78)

Top:
1. Patty played on the softball team.
2. She played hard.
3. She hit two home runs.

Bottom:
1. What time is it?
2. Is it time for lunch?
3. Are you ready to eat?
4. Would you like dessert?

Lesson 58, Using Commas in Lists (P. 79)

Top:
1. I go to work on Monday, Tuesday, Wednesday, Thursday, and Friday.
2. I met with Jenna, Charles, and Ling on Monday.
3. After work I went to the store, the post office, and the dry cleaners.
4. My friend and I ate a pizza topped with mushrooms, pepperoni, and olives.
5. We saw Karen, James, and Janet at home.

Bottom:
1. Pam, Kay, and Juan work hard.
2. Pam sings, dances, and acts in the play.
3. Kay cleans, fixes, and paints the stage.

Lesson 59, Using Commas in Place Names (P. 80)

Top:
1. Akron, Ohio
2. Hilo, Hawaii
3. Macon, Georgia
4. Nome, Alaska
5. Provo, Utah

Bottom:
1. Nancy lives in Barnet, Vermont.
2. Mr. Hill went to Houston, Texas.
3. Did Bruce like Bend, Oregon?
4. Will Amy visit Macon, Missouri?
5. How far away is Salem, Maine?

Lesson 60, Using Commas in Dates (P. 81)

Top:
1. Dec. 12, 1948
2. Mar. 27, 1965
3. Sept. 8, 1994
4. Nov. 1, 1999
5. Jan. 5, 1995

Bottom:
1. Jim was born on August 10, 1967.
2. Jen's birthday is Oct. 17, 1983.
3. Maria visited on February 8, 1991.
4. Dave's party was on July 29, 1993.
5. Carrie started work on Sept. 3, 1994.
6. My driver's license expires on March 17, 1996.
7. Luis bought his car on Oct. 20, 1992.
8. Discuss your answer with your instructor.

Lesson 61, Using Apostrophes in Contractions (P. 82)

Top:
1. were not — weren't
2. was not — wasn't
3. has not — hasn't
4. have not — haven't
5. did not — didn't
6. are not — aren't

Middle:
1. is not
2. do not
3. was not
4. can not
5. did not
6. had not
7. does not
8. are not

Bottom:
1. isn't
2. don't
3. didn't
4. wasn't
5. weren't

Review (P. 83)

The first letter of the following should be circled:
1. grandpa; speedy
2. our; brownie; mittens
3. dr.; atwood; goldie
4. melissa; josé; sunny

1. Mr. W. Bell didn't work on Friday.
2. June isn't a winter month.
3. Is Thanksgiving in November?
4. Wasn't Ms. E. Smith planning the Earth Day activities?

1. Fifth St.
2. Red River Rd.
3. Adams Dr.

1. Mon.
2. Wed.
3. Sat.
4. Tues.
5. Fri.
6. Thurs.

Review (P. 84)

1. July 4, 1990
2. Sept. 5, 1991
3. Jan. 20, 1993
4. Apr. 1, 1994

1. The Joy of Cooking
2. Jurassic Park

1. Trina jumped, ran, and swam to win first place.
2. The seasons are winter, spring, summer, and fall.
3. Dionne lives in Seattle, Washington.
4. This letter is going to Chicago, Illinois.

1. weren't
2. hasn't
3. aren't
4. don't
5. can't
6. isn't

Using What You've Learned (P. 85)

Discuss your answers with your instructor.

Using What You've Learned (P. 86)

Discuss your answers with your instructor.

 Unit 6 Composition

Lesson 62, Writing Sentences (P. 87)

Top, Middle, and Bottom:

Discuss your answers with your instructor.

Lesson 63, Paragraphs (P. 88)

Top:
1. Melinda
2. Melinda is studying for her math test.

Bottom:
1. My wife's birthday
2. Today is my wife's birthday.

Lesson 64, Main Idea (P. 89)

1. Firefighters are brave people.
2. Lenora found that using a computer can be easy.
3. Joe Sanders is a funny man.

Lesson 65, Supporting Details (P. 90)

The first sentence in each paragraph should be circled, and all the other sentences should be underlined.

Lesson 66, Order in Paragraphs (P. 91)

Top:
3
2
4
1

Bottom:
2
3
4
1

Lesson 67, Parts of a Letter (P. 92)

Tell students to fill in the current year.

1. Chris
2. Rose
3. 608 Weston Dr., Markham, Ontario L3R 1E5

Lesson 68, Planning a Letter (P. 93)

Discuss your answers with your instructor.

Lesson 69, Writing a Friendly Letter (P. 94)

The current year should be written.

> 711 Short St.
> Bluff, UT 84512
> Oct. 17, 19___

Dear Pat,

  I just found out some good news. We are moving in June! I will still work at the same place. We are only moving across town.

> Your friend,
> Anna Gomez

Lesson 70, Writing Addresses (P. 95)

Return address:
Miss Anna Gomez
711 Short Street
Bluff, Utah 84512

Address:
Ms. Pat Murray
704 Heard Road
Akron, Ohio 44309

Review (P. 96)

Top and Middle:

Discuss your answers with your instructor.

Bottom:

1. two women who wanted to go to a movie
2. Lauren and Yuko wanted to go to a movie.

Review (P. 97)

Top:

The following sentence should be circled, and all other sentences should be underlined:

I need to clean my apartment this weekend.

Bottom:

The current year should be written. The letters in bold should be circled.

608 Weston Dr.
Markham, Ontario L3R 1E5 } heading
Apr. 12, 19___

greeting→ **d**ear **c**hris,

  I got the job I wrote to you about. I will start next Monday. I am really excited about this job. I think I will really like it. I'll let you know how my first day goes. } body

your friend, ← closing
rose ← name

Using What You've Learned (P. 98)

Discuss your answers with your instructor.

Using What You've Learned (P. 99)

Discuss your answers with your instructor.

1. broken
2. baby
3. the day someone was born

1. forts and castles
2. 12–22
3. 34

Final Reviews

Final Review, Unit 1 (P. 100)

Top:

The following should be done:
1. draw a circle around the box of tissues
2. put an X to the right of the woman's head
3. draw a box above the man's head
4. put an X on the table

Middle:
1. Metric Avenue
2. Park Street
3. 2

Bottom:

The following words should be crossed out:
1. flag
2. bark
3. flower
4. book

Final Review, Unit 2 (P. 102)

1. hold
2. boat
3. pat
4. dirty
5. slow
6. hard
7. glad
8. ill
9. shout
10. hear
11. here
12. here
13. their
14. There
15. there
16. right
17. write
18. right
19. two
20. to
21. to
22. too
23. two

Final Review, Unit 1 (P. 101)

1. 2, 3, 1   angry, chair, hot
2. 1, 3, 2   nest, off, penny

1. poor, quack
2. really, pair

Final Review, Unit 2 (P. 103)

1. a
2. b
3. a
4. a
5. b

6. b
7. a
8. a
9. a
10. b
11. a
12. b

Final Review, Unit 3 (P. 104)

Top:

1. yes
2. no
3. yes
4. no
5. yes
6. no

Middle:

1. Milk was on the table.
2. Butter comes from milk.
3. Cheese also comes from milk.
4. Joanna likes to drink milk.
5. Her son spilled his milk.

Bottom:

1. A
2. T
3. T
4. A
5. T
6. A
7. T
8. T

Final Review, Unit 3 (P. 105)

Top:

1. My family works together to clean the house.
2. Phillip dusts the bookshelves in his room.
3. Katie and Kathy do the laundry.
4. The dirty dishes need to be washed.
5. The house looks very clean now.

Middle:

1. The orange tastes sweet.
2. A lemon smells sour.
3. The sandpaper feels rough.
4. That man sounds angry.
5. The painting looks better over the table.

Bottom:

The words in bold should be circled.

1. **Jerald and Brad** surprised Paula.
2. **The young men** flew into town for the week.
3. **Brad** knocked on Paula's door.
4. **Paula** hugged her two friends.
5. **Some of Paula's neighbors** met her two friends.

Final Review, Unit 4 (P. 106)

1. noun
2. verb
3. noun
4. verb

1. Ms. Grayson
2. Atlanta
3. Georgia

1. trees
2. cars
3. glasses
4. bushes
5. lunches
6. foxes

1. walked
2. working
3. asked
4. dressing
5. helped

Final Review, Unit 4 (P. 107)

Top:
1. ran
2. was
3. saw
4. had
5. I
6. Are
7. played
8. gave
9. an
10. Do

Bottom:
1. They planned a party.
2. It was for Steve's birthday.
3. She invited the guests.
4. We helped put up decorations.
5. He made the cake.
6. He was very surprised.

Final Review, Unit 5 (P. 108)

The letters in bold should be circled.
1. **m**r. **w**. **c**. **s**anchez works at **h**arris **s**chool.
2. **m**r. **k**elly took his class to **r**iverside **p**ark.
3. **t**hey will go to the **h**udson **r**iver in **s**eptember.
4. **w**ill **g**randfather come to see **a**unt **r**uth?
5. **d**id **u**ncle **b**ill come for **t**hanksgiving?
6. **d**onna took a boat ride on **l**ake **e**rie last summer.
7. **d**onna and **i** met **m**s. **h**. **m**. **s**lade last fall.
8. **w**e went to a party for **m**rs. **l**ee in **n**ovember.

1. March — Mar.
2. is not — isn't
3. December — Dec.
4. Saturday — Sat.
5. January — Jan.
6. Sunday — Sun.
7. do not — don't
8. Wednesday — Wed.

1. Hanson Dr.
2. Baker Rd.
3. Second St.

1. Forts and Castles
2. The Firm

Final Review, Unit 5 (P. 109)

1. What will you do in Reno, Nevada?
2. Who is with Dr. Trigo?
3. It is Mr. V. F. Casey.
4. He was born on March 20, 1974.
5. He likes to read, dance, and sing.
6. His family moved there on June 4, 1978.
7. I will be out of town in March, April, and May.
8. Did Ms. Kirkpatrick go to San Francisco, California?
9. The parade will be on New Year's Day.
10. Dr. Nguyen will be in town on Nov. 12.
11. How can we get to Santa Fe, New Mexico?
12. Miss Hall will be late on Monday, Wednesday, and Friday.

Final Review, Unit 6 (P. 110)

Top and Middle:

Discuss your answers with your instructor.

Bottom:

The sentence in bold should be circled, and the other sentences should be underlined.

1.   **Baseball is a sport I like very much.** I like to play on the city team in the summer. I've been saving baseball cards since I was five. I like to watch games at night. I have a great time at the ballpark.

2.   **Richard wanted to look good for his job interview.** The day before the interview he bought some new clothes. He hung his new clothes in the closet so they would not get wrinkled.

Final Review, Unit 6 (P. 111)

Top:

3, 2, 4, 1

Bottom:

Mr. J. T. Conners
4203 Greystone Drive
Cincinnati, OH 45236
      Marla Franklin
      1121 Sunset Road
      Colorado Springs, CO 80919

Check What You've Learned (P. 112)

A. The following should be done:
   1. put an X on the helmet
   2. put an X to the left of the helmet
   3. put an X below the helmet
   4 draw a circle around the helmet

B. 1. south
   2. April Road
   3. east
   4. January Drive
   5. two

Check What You've Learned (P. 113)

C. 1. mud
   2. Tuesday
   3. truck

D. 1. Carlos
      Nadia
      Patty
   2. lake
      ocean
      river

E. 1. key
   2. lamp
   3. jump

F. 1. chop
   2. change
   3. metal

Check What You've Learned (P. 114)

G. 1. rake, run
   2. smooth, tiny
   3. near, asleep

H. 1. too
   2. hear
   3. their

I. The words in bold should be circled.
   1. A, **you**, will swim
   2. T, **Molly**, swims
   3. X

J. The words in bold should be circled.
   1. **Ms. Allison**, works
   2. goes, **Sunday**, **Monday**

K. 1. was
   2. She
   3. an
   4. are

L. The letters in bold should be circled, and punctuation marks should be added as shown.
   1. **c**an you go with **m**s. **m**ary **a**. **b**arnes to a store on **f**irst **s**treet?
   2. **s**he wants to go to a big sale at the store this **f**riday, **s**aturday, and **s**unday.
   3. **w**e didn't find any good bargains there last **a**pril.

M. The sentence in bold should be circled.
   José needed to get to work right away. He got into his car. Then he started the engine and drove to the office. He got to work right on time.